YEARNING FOR MAGIC

THE HEROINE'S JOURNEY SERIES, BOOK 2

The Library of Congress has catalogued publication as follows:

Burch, Melissa, 1961-, author
    Yearning for Magic: Spiritual Journeys of a Mother, Healer, and Lover / Melissa Burch.

ISBN 978-0-9893429-6-4 (paperback)
ISBN 978-0-9893429-9-5 (eBook)

    1. Burch, Melissa, 1961-. 1. Burch, Melissa, 1961-. 2. Travelers' writings, American. 3. Authors, American—21st century—Biography. 4. Spirituality—Biography. I. Title.

Library of Congress Control Number: 2016953564

No part of this book may be reproduced or transmitted in any form, by any means, electronic or mechanical, including photocopying and recording, information storage and retrieval systems, without permission in writing from the publisher, except by a reviewer who may quote a brief passage in a review.

Published by Gaia Press, Claremont, New Hampshire, USA, © 2020

GAIA PRESS, Publishers
Copyright © 2020 Melissa C. Burch

Printed in the United States of America
Cover design by Laura Duffy

GAIA PRESS
425 Washington Street
Claremont, NH 03743
Phone: (617) 491-3374

PRAISE FOR
MY JOURNEY THROUGH
WAR AND PEACE
(THE HEROINE'S JOURNEY, BOOK 1)

"Burch's memoir recounts her remarkable experiences over eight years as a photographer covering the war in Soviet-occupied Afghanistan in the 1980s and as a filmmaker, and also her own personal and spiritual journey as a young woman.... Her accounts provide revealing glimpses into the conflict, Afghan culture, and the dangers of war reporting, particularly for a woman."

– *Publishers Weekly*

"At twenty-two, Melissa Burch headed to Afghanistan with a camera ... determined to film a war for CBS and to find herself. [This] is the dizzying and dazzling account of that journey."

– *Foreword Reviews*

"An absorbing, well-written memoir by a brave adventurer who discovered her own life."

– *Kirkus Reviews*

"Personal growth, international events, the power of images and of individual experience ... Burch's Journey ... [shows] how strange connections can shape the future of both individuals and nations. A great read, highly recommended."

– Davide Mana, *Karavansara Blog*

"Melissa's ... account of travels into Afghanistan, the Soviet Union, and living as a filmmaker in the NYC 80's art scene is intense, raw and enchanting. She has a story that must be told and she does so with a new and charismatic voice."

– Susana Aikin, Emmy Award winning documentary filmmaker of *Transformations*

"Melissa's new life story is not only fascinating, but she had me riveted to every word on the page. Her openness to exploring new horizons ... eliciting meaning out of her experiences, and incorporating the lessons in the next step of her journey are totally relevant to the needs of all of us today."

– Kate Soudant, Editor

Also by Melissa Burch

My Journey Through War and Peace: Explorations of a Young Filmmaker, Feminist and Spiritual Seeker (The Heroine's Journey, Book 1)

The Four Methods of Journal Writing: Finding Yourself Through Memoir

Vital Sensation Manual (Units 1-5)

YEARNING
FOR MAGIC

Spiritual Journeys of a
Mother, Healer, and Lover

Melissa C. Burch

GAIA PRESS

For Leslie Sederlund, who opened her heart to the Burch family

"Magic's just science that we don't understand yet."

~ Arthur C. Clarke

CONTENTS

Preface 1

FIRST PART: ORIGINS

Chapter 1: Baptism 7
Chapter 2: Infertility 17
Chapter 3: Rebirth 35
Chapter 4: Blessings 53

SECOND PART: SYNCHRONICITIES

Chapter 5: Magic 61
Chapter 6: Fascination 73
Chapter 7: Synchronicity 89
Chapter 8: Miracle 105

THIRD PART: PHENOMENA

Chapter 9: Light and Dark Forces 123
Chapter 10: Substances and Spirits 131
Chapter 11: Calamity 145
Chapter 12: Auroville 153

Epilogue: Mystery 165

Acknowledgements 169

About the Author 171

Some details and names have been changed to protect the identities of key players in this memoir or because of imprecise memories.

Many of the opening quotes across the chapters are from Hazrat Inayat Khan, who was a Sufi poet (1882-1927).

PREFACE

"To have courage for whatever comes in life–everything lies in that."
~ Saint Teresa of Ávila

In a recent shamanic journey, while I was in a trance-like state, almost like a dream, I saw a young woman running out of the woods. Chased by men, she headed toward a medieval town square, where they finally caught up with her. She stopped and yelled at them, "You're hurting the people. This must stop." They pilloried her. Her head hung limp in the wooden torture device. Her hands dangled, while another man whipped her. The townspeople watched—not willing to stop the violence.

One of my editors wrote, "[Your story] moves inexorably toward the unbelievable … it will have to be written with great care, or you will lose your readers."

Can I really tell this story in my authentic voice without all the cultural trappings and stereotypes? I've been told since I was a child, "You're forceful, you're strong, you know what you think!" As if this was a bad thing!

This memoir represents a roadmap of my thirties, when I became a mother, learned homeopathy, and connected with spirit as like a lover. I wanted to look beyond daily life and consider phenomena—miracles, things seen and unseen, realities inexplicable and apparently unexplainable.

Reader, your path may have taken you in a totally different direction. Yet, some aspects of my journey may resonate with you. Or you may find these breadcrumbs I share to be a guide, no matter your age or your life circumstances.

The stories are never finished for any of us. I believe we need to hear from brave, powerful, and outspoken women. I stand for HER! The young woman I was when I went to Afghanistan to film the war during the Soviet invasion. The woman I developed into when I became a mother, a homeopath, and a more conscious being. The woman I am who recognizes those parts of myself and their significance.

FIRST PART
ORIGINS

"I have loved in life and I have been loved."

~ Hazrat Inayat Khan

CHAPTER 1

BAPTISM

"I have drunk the bowl of poison from the hands of love as nectar, and have been raised above life's joy and sorrow."

~ Hazrat Inayat Khan

Alex was sleeping in my arms. Wrapped in a small white blanket, he wore a newborn's blue cap from St. Luke's Roosevelt birthing center. His pomegranate-size head, too weighty for him to hold up, was leaning on my shoulder. Together, we entered Agios Nikolaos, the domed Orthodox church in Pyrgos, the Greek village where George and I had been married seven years before.

Pyrgos, paved in white marble, is the largest village on the Cycladic island of Tinos. It is situated just twenty-nine kilometers away from the Panagia Evangelistria church, famous for the annual pilgrimage on August 15th that happens in the port town. Devotees crawl on their hands and knees up the hill from the ferry wharf to the church as a *tama*, an offering or sacrifice in Mary's name, in commemoration of Mother Mary's death and her bodily resurrection before being transported to heaven.

The Agios Nikolaos Church, though much smaller than the church in the Tinos port town, loomed over Pyrgos, standing high up on a hill next to the cemetery where all of George's grandparents were buried. His ancestors' black and white photos looked out from the framed and cherished marble and glass boxes of the graves. When George's parents visited the island from the mainland where they lived, Papa Dimitrakis, the village priest, held a small ceremony for the ancestors, lighting the lamps and praying for their spirits.

Today would be Alex's baptism.

The hot summer sun streamed through the skylight in the vaulted sky blue church ceiling and was reflected on the chessboard black and white marble floor. The large, standing shiny brass candlestick holders and chandeliers were candleless. Instead, thin white eighteen-inch candles were lit for the baptism and held by Alex's two young cousins, George's brother's boys, while their two younger sisters looked on.

Members of my family, who had arrived from the States, cheerful in anticipation of celebrating Alex's birth, gathered around me inside the sun-streaked entrance. I felt proud and exuberant in my new role as mother.

George and I had loved the marriage ritual that had brought our American and Greek families together here for the first time. In ancient times, Poseidon, the Greek God also known as the island's protector, was worshipped on Tinos as the "Great Doctor." Poseidon had sent a flock of storks to rid the island of snakes. The God of the Sea had brought sunshine and safe travels for everyone on both occasions, our wedding and now our son's baptism. Ancient and personal history danced together on this island.

I grew up isolated in a dysfunctional nuclear family where my parents fought constantly about money and infidelity. For me, marriage had been a "never-would-I-dare-do-that." My parents' conflicted relationship and ultimate divorce had left an imprint on me. But after ten years of a long-distance relationship with George, we wanted a big celebration to bring our families together. The church ceremony grounded us in a tradition I was unfamiliar with, especially the religious aspect of sanctifying our betrothal as a union in the eyes of God. Yet the Greek wedding was our chance to do it all differently, to be in a relationship that embraced the depth of spirit, joy, and communion in the real world. Now, my fears of marriage had long washed away after many happy years.

And here I was again, among familiar faces. Papa Dimitrakis

had chanted our wedding vows in ecclesiastic Greek. Elpitha, George's first cousin and my only bridesmaid, would now be Alex's godmother. She had stood by my side at the wedding, translating the instructions into English. Elpitha told me when to circle the altar while she held the *stefana*, the two wedding crowns, connected by a ribbon over George's and my head. The ribbon symbolized that we were bound together in our new family. And the crowns symbolized the nobility of our marriage. We would be king and queen of our household. Then, Elpitha told me to step on George's toe, at the priest's command that I obey my husband. She had explained before the service the significance of this Greek ritual: By stepping on his toe, I would be the dominant partner. At the ceremony, George sidestepped my protest to the church order, and I was unable to step on his foot. The congregation laughed.

Before our wedding, the priest had requested that George and I produce a document from my church, stating that I was a virgin and had never been married before. Because I had been baptized and confirmed in the Episcopal Church as a teenager—a ritual that didn't make me particularly religious—a friend introduced us to an Episcopal priest in Brooklyn, who was comfortable executing documents to help his immigrant parishioners. He was the great-great-grandson of one of the signers of the Declaration of Independence and procured a piece of parchment that he wrote on with a quill and ink. The Episcopal priest knew I was already married to George in a civil marriage the year before and for sure, at twenty-eight, was not a virgin. He stamped the paper with the church seal in red wax, and George had the document officially translated at the Greek embassy. The Episcopal priest had left out the virgin part and had written in old English that I was not married in the eyes of God. My just-in-case baptism (arranged by my atheist mother, in case there was a God after all) had paid off in the end, enabling me to be married in the Greek Orthodox church.

* * *

"George, is there anything I need to know about the baptism?" I had asked before we made the plans with the village priest to baptize Alex.

"No, I don't think so. All kids go through this. It's a normal rite of passage," he said.

"Are you sure?"

He nodded.

"It'll be something like our wedding," he said.

I trusted the tradition to take care of us. Most of the service and its rituals would be incomprehensible to me, and only after the baptism did I find out what all the symbols and chanting were about.

The priest, Papa Dimitrakis, robed in grey cotton and white silk-embroidered vestments, motioned for all of us to step closer to the altar at the back of the church.

My father, in a white linen suit and topped off with an Italian straw hat, his second wife, in a linen blue dress, their nine-year-old daughter in a frilly dress, my sister and brother and their families all dressed in their Sunday best, other relatives, our European American clan, clustered together far from the double front doors of the church and the bright sunlight. George's parents, his brother, his German sister-in-law, their children, and his cousins stood shoulder to shoulder with my family. Spiro, George's father, patted my father's back. George's mother, Antigone, hugged me, careful not to wake Alex.

The priest stood, hands folded in prayer, by the baptism font, a large bronze basin representing the Divine womb. He wore thick glasses poised at the end of his nose and a black cap on his bald head. His pointy beard was white and wiry. Papa Dimitrakis had presided over our wedding, George's grandparents' funerals, and the baptisms of George's brother's four children.

The priest lit the frankincense at the base of the baptism font. Twirls of smoke floated over the empty basin. The sweet, spicy aroma filled the village church. George stood next to me, his smaller frame and boyish looks made it hard to believe he was the father of our son. He dressed casually in black chino pants and a t-shirt. My outfit was more formal, a floral skirt and white silk blouse, adorned with a long beaded necklace, a gift from George's mother, and comfortable black sandals. Eleni, the church elder and village *yaya*—grandmother—took Alex, who was still sleeping, from my arms and brought him to the priest. She cradled him as Papa Dimitrakis breathed three times on his face and signed the cross as many times on his forehead.

"... I lay my hand upon this, Thy servant Alexander Spiro, who has been accounted worthy to seek refuge in Thy Holy Name and safekeeping under the shelter of Thy wings," said the priest in Greek, welcoming Alex.

The church recognized the individuality of a child by his unique name, an expression of dignity in the eyes of God. I smiled in the bright light that streamed through the church entrance, left open for villagers to wander in and out. Alex and I were joining a community that had deep roots and love for their flock.

When Alex's name was spoken out loud in the church, Spiro looked over at me. His sculptured features showed every emotion as he pursed his lips, a gesture of disapproval. Spiro had been avoiding me all morning. I had insisted on the forbidden—to give our child my last name and not his father's Greek last name, Papargyris. Spiro was Alex's middle name, and we planned to call him Spiro whenever we were in Greece.

I was afraid of the possibility that Alex would be conscripted into the Greek military (as his father had been), and it was my feeble attempt to make sure that didn't happen. I had met a Greek American who told me he had been forced to serve in the army during one of the Turkish skirmishes when he visited Greece as a tourist. George denied the reality of this story, but he did agree to give Alex my last name, not for fear of the Greek military but because my last name, Burch, was easier to say and spell for Americans. But in this village, where everyone knew each other's names, name giving was more about patriarchal pride than God's acceptance.

Icons of Saint Nicholas and the Virgin Mary hung behind the ceremonial spot. Elpitha stepped up next to the priest and faced west, where the sun set and toward the location of Hades and the gates of Hell. As the sponsor, she was bestowed an important role that dated back to Roman times. As a godparent, she was entrusted to raise the child in the Christian church should we, the parents, die. The baptizing was meant to create a spiritual bond between them, and the obligation was an honor not meant to be taken lightly. The church matron, Eleni, carefully handed the sleeping child to Elpitha. Alex woke up crying.

The priest began the first step of the baptism, the exorcism—the journey from evil into the light of love.

Elpitha was called upon by the priest to renounce Satan: "Be afraid, come out, and depart from this creature, and return not, neither hide thy self in him, nor encounter him, nor operate in him, or influence him."

Alex wailed louder.

"... but get thee hence to thine own Hell." the priest expelled the devil from Alex's innocent being. I never thought my son was possessed by the devil. I didn't even believe in the devil. The service was all in Greek so I had no idea what the priest was chanting.

Priest and godmother turned and faced east, and the priest chanted, "Christ, who is the light of the world ... and worthy of the great grace of Thy Holy Baptism." Alex was accepted by Christ.

George held Alex's tiny, white-socked feet. I stroked his capped head. Alex wailed louder, and Elpitha rubbed his back. Alex was no longer a child of the body, but a child of God's kingdom.

"*Kyrie eleison.*" Lord have mercy, said the priest.

"Whaa, whaa, whaaaaaaa," Alex cried.

I took Alex from Elpitha's arms, removed the cap, and rocked him in our familiar bounce. He calmed in my arms.

The priest lit Alex's white baptismal candle, a symbol of the light of Christ, which was meant to be lit at his future wedding and at his funeral, a final way to aid the soul to meet its judgment. At the final judgment, God would decide if the soul went to Heaven or Hell.

Eleni guided me behind the nave, in the shadow of the church, to undress Alex. The removal of his clothes signified the casting off of the old slough of sin. George handed the priest a recycled plastic water bottle filled with local olive oil. The priest blessed the oil in the name of the Father, Son, and Holy Spirit.

Then, the Greek chanting began. I was holding Alex in my arms. Elpitha grabbed him from me. Alex started wailing again. I went to take him back. We had a tug of war. The chanting droned on. But I was losing. Elpitha was stronger than me. She pulled Alex out of my arms and stood close to the priest, far away from me. The idea that Elpitha would raise our son if George and I died was far from my consciousness at this point. I only wanted to cradle and comfort him.

The priest poured the oil of "gladness" on his arthritic fingers, a divine influence meant to be holy, emanating spirit, power, or God. Then, he spoke and touched Alex's ears, "to hear words of faith," his mouth, "shall speak wisdom," his stomach, "for healing of soul and body," his feet, "to walk in your footsteps, casting out serpents and scorpions, and all the power of the enemy," his hands, "made for me," and finally his back, "for whoever wishes to come after me, let him deny himself and follow me."

Looking back at the meaning of the baptism, why would anyone deny themselves? Was Alex meant to trust the church more than his intuition? What was meant by follow? Follow whom? Christ, God, our Savior? But the Greek words held no meaning for me. All I knew was that the service was disturbing Alex.

Alex cried in rhythmic cycles catching his breath before repeating the refrain, "whaaaa." With the tears of a newborn facing the real world, Alex protested loudly, powerless to stop the ritual.

George picked up the yellow plastic pail and poured the warm water into the baptismal font. His motions were automatic, oblivious to my battle raging with Elpitha over our child.

I took Alex back. His face awash with tears, he gulped, then took a breath, and finally stopped crying. I breathed for the first time since he was taken away from me. I relaxed my shoulders. All eyes were on me. The chanting continued and then Elpitha grabbed him, stealth-like, again and handed him to the tall commanding priest. The ceremony was indomitable. There was no place for me to stop the ritual and discuss what was happening.

The priest opened the silver-covered bible and read, "For this water, that it may be sanctified by the might, operation, and descent of the Holy Spirit ..." He seemed unperturbed by the freaked-out baby.

Alex's hands made little fists and his legs pulled up tight to his body, as the priest held him naked facing his family then dunked him three times in the basin of water. He emerged wet from head to toe and was handed to Elpitha, who wrapped a towel around his screaming body.

This church was torturing him. I wrestled Elpitha and grabbed him. I won this round, but then she surprised me and took him from behind.

The wailing now was a scream, a sound he had never made before, not even when his colic was at its worst, two weeks after his birth. His face had gone red.

The priest cut three locks of Alex's brown hair, while Alex shrieked in Elpitha's arms. His hair was meant to be Alex's gift to the church on this August day in 1997. The irony of a gift not freely given did not escape me.

When would this torture stop? For forty-five minutes, tiny Alex howled. George had been darting between Elpitha and me, helping the priest. When he saw the pain on my face, no Alex in my arms, he stood next to me as we watched our child cry, his needs ignored for the sake of orthodoxy. I was furious at the church dogma that required this ritual. I had approached this event as if we were going to a party, but I felt an outsider to this religion that believed in original sin. It made no sense. Devils do not live in babies.

Now, Alexander Spiro Burch had been accepted as a cleansed soul by the church, his sins washed away. He could take sacraments now, which according to the Greek Orthodox Church would reveal God to him. After the final line of the chant was recited, Alex would be listed in the church book as a Greek Orthodox. Elpitha handed Alex back to me. I consoled him, and he quieted in my arms.

CHAPTER 2

INFERTILITY

"My heart, aflame in love, set afire every heart that came in touch with it."

~ Hazrat Inayat Khan

In New York City, on the fifth floor of the Beth Israel Medical Center, in the Chief of Urology's office overlooking Union Square, George and I nervously awaited our verdict. Dr. Evans in his white overcoat with a blue pinstripe Brooks Brothers button-down shirt showing underneath, sat behind an ultra-modern metal and glass desk as he pronounced his judgment:

> One in a million chances for you two to get pregnant. I know this is not the news you wanted to hear, but it is the truth. George's sperm count is low, but the real problem is their morphology. Irregular, curving tails, absent heads, severely abnormal shapes.

I gasped. It was 1995. I had spent the last nine months on a mission to become pregnant. Dr. Evans was the fourth doctor we had seen. George had been reluctant to have a child but was willing to pursue this medical avenue to please me. After researching the best doctor for our case, we found one who happened to be the most expensive and also outside of our insurance HMO. On our way out, we would write a check equal to our monthly rent.

"What about the varicocele? The last urologist, Dr. Rosa Miguel told us if George has an operation, it will correct the problem," I asked.

"Not true," Dr. Evans said. "This is a controversial procedure and does not result in a cure."

I had come to the same conclusion, but had sought out Dr. Evans for a second opinion. It was a condition similar to a varicose vein, but instead of being in a leg it was in a man's scrotum. George sank back in the retro Hamilton armchair. Tears formed in his eyes.

"Are you saying that if we had followed Dr. Miguel's recommendation, George would have gone through an operation that would have left him scarred and with no chance of improving his fertility?"

"Yes, most probably," Dr. Evans said confidently.

* * *

Two weeks before, Dr. Rosa Miguel, dressed in a white overcoat with a stethoscope stuffed in her breast pocket, had sat on an office rolling chair opposite George and me, in her cramped, windowless, fluorescent-lit office. The disinfectant smell, sealed instruments, bandages, and a framed poster of a Bahamas beach at sunset were in sharp contrast to Dr. Evans's high-end office with a lithograph print of a tall ship next to his Harvard Medical School diploma. Our five-minute visit with Dr. Miguel felt rushed compared to the relaxed manner in which Dr. Evans spoke to us. But this visit was covered by our HMO insurance and didn't cost us a penny.

Up until this time, I thought doctors knew how to fix the body like car mechanics fixed cars, but the more I learned, the more I started to doubt. The World Wide Web became my tool for researching infertility. The disagreement between doctors on varicocele and fertility was the beginning. In the '90s, the view on infertility was that it was almost always the woman's fault, which was not true in my case.

Before I turned to my general practitioner, I had spent six months reading on the web and following the recommended ways to get pregnant naturally, but George and I had no results. Based on my research, we used a thermometer to determine my ovulation, paid attention to my mucous, and had sex based on my menstruation cycles, which were regular and twenty-eight days apart. We had sex several days in a row when my mucous was egg-white sticky and estrogen levels were at their highest, peak fertility days. My egg could only live for one day. The average length of the journey to the fallopian tubes is 175 millimeters, which meant the road runners of the sperm team could potentially get there in 45 minutes. In practice, it could take up to three days.

When the OB/GYN, our second doctor after my primary physician referred me, heard of the steps George and I took to get pregnant, she had me go to the lab several times for blood tests to check my hormone levels, the first step in an infertility diagnosis. My periods were normal but, according to medical procedure, blood tests were the gold standard of what was really happening in the body. Once my hormone level test came back normal from the labs, I was promoted up the chain to more specialized doctors and more invasive testing.

I laid on a metal gurney, naked, with a white sheet covering me in a factory-like room. Five other women were waiting for the same procedure on their hard beds. I was injected with methylene blue dye through my cervix to see if I had endometriosis, the second step in a diagnosis. My tubes were not blocked, and the dye spilled into the abdomen. Again, I was declared medically able to produce a baby.

Now my OB/GYN suggested my husband be tested. This was something I had been advocating all along, but without a referral from the HMO insurance company, we could not be reimbursed.

* * *

When we left Dr. Evans's office on 14th Street, we took a circuitous route back to the Penington Friends House, a Quaker community on East 15th Street, where we lived. We circled Gramercy Park several times. The tall, black iron fence with decorative spears guarded actor Edwin Booth's statue, which stood imperious behind the locked, arched wrought-iron gates that kept this private park out of reach. George and I did not have a key, a privilege awarded to residents that lived on the authentic gas-lit street surrounding the park. We lived a few blocks from this park and would have loved to have access to the garden. So we kept circling the park, instead.

"Next step is for us to make an appointment at a fertility clinic. Dr. Evans said our only hope is the ICSI IVF," I said, ready to take on the next plan of action in this battle for motherhood.

"I don't know if we want this intra-cytoplasmic sperm injection. We'd be having a test tube baby. Dr. Evans didn't give us good odds for this procedure, and I doubt our insurance company will pay for this." George was backtracking.

It was hard to believe that this whole complicated process could work. It would entail harvesting my eggs, isolating four healthy sperms, injecting one sperm into each egg, then waiting two to three days. If all went well with the fertilized eggs, the embryos would be transferred into my womb. According to the medical literature on the web, the success rate for this procedure was not high: 1 out of 19 chances. And I could have quadruplets, if all the eggs made it! At least medical technology was giving us a chance.

The drive to procreate came from a well of emotions, mostly unexamined until now. The summer before we began the infertility odyssey, I had felt a major shift. On the face of it, it was precipitated by a difficult case of pneumonia with a hacking cough so persistent that it woke me up every night all through the spring. When I recovered, I saw babies everywhere on the streets of Manhattan. Where had they been hiding? I wanted to touch them, hold them, play with them, care for them. I stared into their faces. Some turned away from me then looked back. Some giggled. Some had wise faces. Some were dimply. Others were squishable. I had baby fever, a kind of baby mania took hold of me. And I was enthralled!

The sun was setting, but George and I continued around the park. George wanted a more natural process.

"But Melissa, this sounds crazy. You're not really the mother type. You know how all your friends have pointed out your workaholic tendencies and their concerns that you wouldn't be a good mother," he said. We were walking home now.

"What!" I shouted. "Really, do you know how much that hurts what you're saying? Do you really believe it?"

"Maybe we're not meant to have kids after all."

"But I could be a good mother! You and my friends are dead wrong. I want a baby. I want to be a mother." Tears streamed down my cheeks.

I was sure George was deflecting. He was the problem! I wanted to tell him how inept he was as a man, but I couldn't stoop so low. I had seen his tears in the doctor's office.

* * *

At a Greek diner, I met Julie, a friend ten years older than me whom I consulted whenever I faced new challenges. She was a single woman who didn't have any children. We sipped our lukewarm coffee and shared a slice of cheesecake, while I told her about all the various tests George and I had been through.

"Maybe it's not for you. You're always working ... Motherhood is not for everyone," she said. "And George isn't into it, either. And he's really not the breadwinner type."

She was talking about George's part-time jobs—repairing organs in churches, maintaining the audio/visual department at Beth Israel Medical Center, and being an assistant manager at the Penington. None of the jobs gave benefits or opportunities for advancement. In Greece, he had been a sailor, a baker, ran a hardware store ...

"Yes, but it means so much to me. I want to be a mother," I said.

"You don't have to subject yourself to all these doctors. You could make another film."

"Christine told me the same thing," I said about a mutual girlfriend. "Actually, she said I wouldn't make a great mother because I work too much."

Were my friends just trying to console me because George

and I were having trouble getting pregnant? I understood where they were coming from; I really didn't seem the mother type. I was focused on my next film project and spent all my time working. If I wasn't working, I was meditating or going to spiritual weekend retreats. Up until this point, I never really had the urge to have babies. But something in me had changed. Now, I knew that I wanted a family.

* * *

The child George and I had aborted in Greece over a decade ago was often on my mind. After years of wearing a diaphragm and putting spermicides inside it, I couldn't believe how the abortion came back to haunt me.

When I was twenty years old, on a Sunday in late summer in Athens, George and I walked through the polluted city's crowded streets, narrowed further by the cars parked on sidewalks leaving only tight paths for pedestrians. We walked up to the Acropolis, down to the Agora Roman Forum, across to Panathinaiko, the ancient stadium, oblivious to their magnificence. The night was hot. The smog of the city covered the stars, and a diffused grey glow overhung above us.

"Paps Mou, is this the time to start a family?" I asked George. Paps Mou was short for his last name Papargyris.

I answered my own question, "I'm twenty years old. I hate marriage. Look at my parents. They made a total mess of it." I was crying now. "Something's wrong with me—I'm lacking in some fundamental way. It's deep. I'm not sure where it comes from, but it's there. Even when you make love to me, it's there, this hole, this never good enough, this hollow pit."

George squeezed me tight. I could smell his Polo cologne on his neck, a woodsy evergreen scent.

"Melissa, it's your decision. I want you. I love you."

"And I'm fat. Can you imagine how fat I'll be pregnant?"

"Melissa, I don't care. You're beautiful. I love you."

"I hate hospitals!" was my final complaint.

My mother had wanted it all, the career, the husband, the family, and it was a disaster. She was the first woman economist at the Federal Reserve Board, raising three children without much help in Washington, D.C. Then she became an alcoholic, after my father nearly died in a fire. She felt obligated to run my father's business when he was injured. It was too much. I didn't believe it was possible to succeed on all fronts. Something would have to be sacrificed. I wanted a chance to be a filmmaker and to be with George. The thought of adding a child was unthinkable. The balance would implode, and the child would be the victim. Or I would end up like my mother, depressed, angry, or worst of all, an alcoholic.

George made all the arrangements through a dentist friend. He used his savings from the photo sales of his coverage of the war in Afghanistan. He paid for a civilized, but illegal abortion in a hospital clinic, which looked more like a modern gynecologist's office than a sterilized surgery room. Following the procedure, I woke up after the anesthesia wore off in a simple dull green room on a metal cot. Five jabbering Greek women were recovering on similar beds in the room with me; their voices pierced my skull. George, the only man in the room, held my hand. I wanted to know what these women were saying.

"No, it's OK. You're fine, rest," George comforted me.

"No, tell me what they're saying."

Whispering, he translated, "That son of a bitch, should have killed him when I could ... Bastard, leaving me here like this ... Piece of shit, who does he think he is? Asshole, has a wife and four kids ..."

Now, thirteen years later, I wondered if I had made a mistake. What if that was our only chance to have a child? I didn't believe in sin, but maybe there really was a vengeful God out there. In my heart, I felt like I was being punished.

* * *

Living at the Penington, a four-floor brownstone next door to the Quaker Meeting House, on a quiet street near Union Square, meant we were part of a multi-generational community. I worked there as the bookkeeper, one of my many part-time jobs, to support my filmmaker life. When George came to New York, after a stretched out, ten-year, long-distance relationship, we decided that this intentional community in lower Manhattan would be our new home.

We had spent most of our relationship apart. We had met at film school in London, when I was eighteen. I left him a month after we got together to work for a film producer in D.C. He went to Afghanistan as a war journalist for the BBC. I followed his course and spent two years in and out of Afghanistan for CBS, while he was drafted into the Greek navy. Then, we finally tried to be together in New York City, but I was living with a woman. For five more years I bounced back and forth visiting him in Greece—wanting him and never letting him go. He agreed to try again.

George longed for a community like his ancestors' village. My yearning was based on a lack of any family community—my father's grandparents, my parents, and my siblings now scattered in different states. I felt fulfilled by this community, with friendships solidified over shared dinners. The house was full, with thirty residents and friends spilling out into the community spaces. Our room, number 24, was the only private place George and I could talk. Twenty-four in numerology added up to 6, the Lovers' number. But, as we considered having a child, we felt like adversaries instead. In our small room, which could be crossed in six steps, we climbed the ladder to the loft bed to find the lover's harmony once more.

We leaned against big down pillows, pulled the cotton comforter tight around us, and stared out the narrow window opposite us. French lace curtains that George's mother had made for us framed the view. It took painstaking work to make them—teeny, tiny knots, culminating in a beautiful pattern. Every house on the Greek island had these decorative curtains on their windows. They transported me back to the island of Tinos.

"We don't have the money; we don't have secure jobs—the kind to raise a family on. We wouldn't have the freedom we have now to do what we want when we want. It's a big step in our lives and, frankly, we're not ready," George said.

George was not career driven. He took jobs that came his way. He worked hard but was not ambitious. He preferred to seek out kindness in relationships. He wanted to help people, listen to their problems, fix their computers, enjoy a movie together.

"I am ready. I want this more than anything in the world," I said. "We've always had the money for whatever we wanted. Why would it be any different now?"

I saw myself as a mother. I was compelled to become pregnant.

"You wanted to study energy medicine, and you took the job washing the pots after dinner at the Penington so you could pay for the workshops," I said. "There's always a way if you want something bad enough."

"But a child is much more expensive and a forever decision," he said.

"I'm working at Dillon Read full time, we have benefits, insurance, and some stability now," I said. I worked as an assistant to the IT manager of a financial institution, and my boss supported my using the company fax machine, computer, and phone to produce my television series about women's lives.

George was reluctant to change our lives so drastically, but after months of these discussions, safe up in our loft bed nest, George wanted to please me. We would make love to procreate. I did not insert the diaphragm. High up off the ground, we were making new life. We made love every day for a week. Then, my mucous was stickier and white, a sign of fertility. We made love during those next four days, too. We were enjoying the freedom of the body, enveloped in each other.

I added up the months. Ten months from conception I would deliver our child. It was late August so, by June, a Cancer child would be with us.

Yet, ten days after all this manic sex, my period came right on schedule. My clockwork periods brought back the usual painful, terrible cramps, bloating, and now a foul mood. George had learned acupressure from a book. He applied pressure on specific points on my body, on my lower back, right calf, and above my bellybutton, which made my flow gentler and reduced the pain. And I took less ibuprofen than usual.

But why was I not pregnant, yet? I started reading about how to get pregnant. It could take two or three months of trying.

Apparently, this was totally normal. So we waited until I ovulated, the sticky substance a pure giveaway that I was fertile. We had sex four or five times during those four days. Then, I would fantasize about the baby, who would now be a Leo, passionate and the center of attention. I thought I would take six weeks off so we could take the baby to Tinos in August.

And each month my period came right on time. The hard cramps a reminder of the failure. My love-at-first-sight of babies turned to envy of their mothers. I felt cheated, but medicine and science would have the answers. I was sure.

The only success in my life at that time that mattered to me was my weight loss. Used to being plump, I kept a strict diet and exercise routine and dropped to my lowest weight ever: 145 pounds. My weight was one thing I could control. I focused obsessively on being thin. Each month, I charted the two- to four-pound weight loss, asking George to take a Polaroid of me in my black bathing suit so I could see my body changing. I was getting slimmer instead of rounder, as I realized I was not able to conceive.

While I read books on pregnancy and infertility, and arranged new doctor appointments, George went to his energy healing school. He studied with Levent Bolukbasi, a Turkish man that had worked with Barbara Brennan, someone I never heard of but who, according to George, was a major healer in the United States. George didn't want to be a professional healer, he just wanted to help people. This course of study was his hobby and had nothing to do with real medicine. I could not take any of this woo woo science seriously. I dismissed his training as an activity for mostly bored rich women looking to be entertained.

Yet George had always been fascinated with channeling, occult practices, and new age prophets. He wanted to figure out a way to connect to the Divine and to communicate with Source in a two-way connection. I was a daily meditator and, through my Gurdjieffian spiritual teacher and group, honed my internal observation practices. George Gurdjieff was an Armenian guru from the early 20th century who developed a method to reach a higher state of consciousness. My teacher was a direct descendant from his esoteric school. However, I could not see any connection between my spiritual work and what George was interested in. They seemed worlds apart.

* * *

I took the elevator up to the 20th floor. In a small room, gathered in a circle of metal chairs, seven women, including the grey haired Jewish therapist who looked like a grandmother, sat together for the fertility support group. I was a few minutes late and took the last empty seat.

"How was your week?" asked the therapist.

"I haven't had my period for years, but it came after the hormone shots. I guess I should be grateful," Ellen said, who looked as old as the therapist.

"I'm still recovering after the miscarriage last month. My doctors want me to wait before I try again with another insemination," said Lauri, a woman dressed in a power suit.

"Have any of you screamed at your partner? I can't believe how crazy those hormone shots make me. I could strangle the super for not holding the door for me," said Martha, a tall and anorexic looking woman.

Most of the women seemed desperate because they no longer trusted their bodies and had put all their hopes in technology—and it was failing them. Some of the women were on their third round of IVF, in vitro fertilization in a test tube. None of them became pregnant while I attended the weekly meetings. Most of them were ten years older than me, their wrinkles, a sign that their menopause was right around the corner, which added to their desperation. I was the youngest in the group and a beginner on the infertility treatment road.

* * *

At this time, I was working as a personal assistant at Dillon Read where I had plenty of time on the job to research how to get pregnant. I felt like a journalist again; I gathered as much information as I could, then made game plans. My insurance was not giving us a clear go-ahead for the ICSI IVF. Each round would cost $10,000. Our HMO would give us two chances, at the most, and they had yet to send the paperwork to the fertility clinic to start the procedure. I decided to turn to my family for help.

I called my father, who was making more and more money from his software business and had the means to help us.

"I can't get the insurance company to agree for us to start," I said. "I can't wait another month, it's killing me."

"I understand. Don't worry about the money, just send me the bills. I'll pay them," he said.

"Thank you, thank you. This means the world to me," I hung up the phone.

George and I took the PATH train then a bus to the Jersey City fertility clinic, an hour-and-a-half commute to the only clinic that would accept checks. This was the one place that agreed to do ICSI IVF without insurance. My father agreed to pay for whatever it cost.

"You'll be getting hormone shots several times a day for eight to ten days depending on what your doctor prescribed," a nurse told us.

These hormone shots were meant to activate a rush of eggs to descend during my ovulation so they could be harvested for the IVF procedure. The nurse showed George how to take the sterile needle, rub the spot at the top of my thigh and on my butt with the alcohol swab, remove the cap from the fat needle, pinch a large area of my skin, and then inject the hormone at a forty-five-degree angle. He was to hold the syringe at the site for ten to fifteen seconds and then swiftly withdraw it. George practiced on an orange, while I worried about all the side effects of these injections that I had heard about from the women in my support group. The bloating, the mood swings, and the counting of days after ovulation would take over my life.

I started having stomach pains, sore breasts, and depression. And the truth was I started feeling depressed even before my first shot. My period would be controlled by birth control pills to regulate my already regular periods. My natural body cycles, which often followed the moon, would now be drug induced. I would do anything, even take four shots a day, if it meant I could get pregnant. I was the healthy one, but I would have the most invasive treatments. George would have to masturbate into a cup. The lab technician would take his semen, extract the sperm, and insert them into my harvested eggs for the ICSI procedure.

George became a foot soldier, the doctors his commanders. He showed none of the obsession I had when I saw babies in strollers or when I heard about friends getting pregnant and, worse still, when I was invited to a baby shower. My pain felt intolerable, as many women around me were getting pregnant—some without even trying.

Yet George understood the depth of my suffering; he was the only one who did. We talked over and over all the details of the procedures. One day I grieved when I bled after my period came two days late. All the insurance paperwork drove me nuts. Most of all, I hoped that the next moon cycle would bring me a cherub. These roller coaster feelings were too hard to expose to anyone else, but George was always willing to listen. With each twist and turn of our journey, his equanimity grew.

We talked about names. His love of spoonerisms turned every name into a private word game for us—Stacy was too hasty, Michael rode a bicycle, Mary was hairy. He could make me laugh, as he warmed to the idea of becoming a father.

After my OB/GYN recommended that George be tested, his only complaint was that he felt unmanly ejaculating into a cup, aided by the latest issues of Playboy in a closet-like room in the infertility clinic. The worst part of it was when he handed his semen to the same nurse who had brought him the pornographic magazines with the cup. He was totally embarrassed by the chore.

Then, I found out that the reason the insurance company was hesitating was they wanted George and me to go through two inseminations before the more invasive and expensive in-vitro procedures. I was infuriated. Those cryptic HMO rules!

* * *

During this year of infertility testing, I never gave up on the possibility of an immaculate conception. I had rarely prayed in my life; now I prayed for God to intervene just this once and make me pregnant. Deep in my unconscious, I had a bit of my mother's philosophy: "Just in case it was true." Maybe God granted favors if you asked. I would pray for a child.

On our last summer vacation to Tinos, a month before I became pregnant, we purchased the tin-plated card of a baby from the Tinos church, a sacred place. Greek Orthodox believers crawled on their hands and knees to the Tinos church after they were granted their wishes: a husband, a healthy baby, better eyesight, safe travels. They climbed up the steep road to the large church on the hill with a carved marble bell tower, then finally up a broad white marble staircase to kiss the gold and jeweled icon inside the left side of the nave. Such a practical religion. Devotees paid their penance after receiving their miracles. I prepared myself mentally for the climb up to Panagia Evangelistria, the church of the Virgin Mary, on our hands and knees, if needed, to honor our successful request.

We kept having sex when I ovulated. It was a desperate kind of sex, mechanical, scheduled. After sex, I would prop my butt up high, imagining the one great athlete, the hero sperm making the journey to the moon, finding my egg, pulling into its orbit to make life. We tried the turkey baster, gave the sperm a running start, and saved them a few sperm miles of their great journey. Even that didn't work.

Meanwhile, George's younger brother, Marios, was having his fourth child. It all seemed so unfair. And I was taken aback by his seeming foolishness, as he announced the arrival of yet another child with a sheepish grin and feigning surprise at how it had happened. Maybe I should get inseminated by Marios? He obviously had good sperm, and the gene pool would be the same. Or should we go to a sperm bank? Or should we adopt?

I wanted the experience of pregnancy and giving birth. After sixteen months of trying, I wanted this rite of passage more than ever.

At this point, George had eighteen months of energy healing training and told me he was ready to graduate from The IM School of Healing Arts. But what did that mean? There would be a final thesis where each student would work with one classmate and cure them! I laughed at the absurdity. We had been in ten months of treatment and not once did it dawn on him or me that his school could be a healing center for infertility. He became serious. He would be in treatment now with Dan, George's IM schoolmate, and George was certain he would be cured with Dan's help.

They met over the next two weeks. Dan laid his hands on George, spun his chakras, raked energy fields, shifted invisible energy up and down his body, moving his hands in wavelike gestures, bringing Source and any angels who cared to help to aid him.

Energy healing was a form of alternative medicine, where the healer would channel healing energy into the patient to produce spontaneous remissions of different diseases. Most scientists had concluded that this was purely a placebo effect, though that in itself was nothing to shrug at. Placebos can have as high as a 40% success rates, as stated by the National Institutes of Health, without any of the horrible side effects of conventional medicine.

* * *

We scheduled the insemination based on my exact ovulation schedule—not one day off of scheduled sex. I tested my urine, examined my mucous, and measured my temperature. I took the afternoon off from my job at Dillon Read on the day of the procedure. I sat on a bench in Central Park waiting for George to arrive with the test tube full of his sperm.

George arrived a little bit late, while I took in this glorious September day, its blue skies, and a fresh breeze that rustled the trees. The pond in the distance had a family of ducks waddling behind its mother. George told me he felt strange being in the lab. The lab was in a gothic building, with oak paneling and the strangest people, a midget, a giant, and no women around—not one nurse. The place and its subpar lighting spooked him. George had wondered if he had the right address. He handed the cup with his sperm to the lab technician, whom he described as a giant man with a square jaw and forehead who wearing round spectacles. This Frankenstein-like technician tested the semen, washed, spinned and returned it in a test tube.

"He said my sperm count was off the charts. Yes, he had never seen such a high one," George said. "I told you the healing work Dan and I did would cure me." He handed me the white paper bag with his übersperm-count semen, which the doctor would artificially inject into me to make our baby.

I wanted to believe. Could energy healing really work? I

remembered the odds Dr. Evans gave us. Was there a possibility of a mystery I didn't understand?

We carried our thick folder of documents to the infertility clinic, all the tests in order by gender and dates. I wore my lucky black linen suit with a pink blouse, gifts my mother had given me before she died. At the clinic, I undressed and put on the cotton pink gown. I climbed up on the examining table and put my feet in the metal stirrups as George held my hand. This was not the way babies were meant to be conceived, but it was our way in the modern era. A medical instrument that looked like a metal turkey baster was filled with George's sperm that had already gone for a spin around the galaxy.

The doctor looked like the mother of one of the residents at the Penington, a déjà vu. I felt comforted to be in the care of a doctor I recognized, even though I had never met her before: a synchronicity that made me feel we were in good hands for this procedure. We kept asking her for her name because we were sure we had met before. Strange. OK, she asked me to take several deep breaths. She inserted the cold instrument between my legs and up high into my uterus. She told me to lie on the table and not to move for the next thirty minutes while the sperm ran their marathon.

George hovered close to me. He kissed me, brushed my hair away from my eyes. He held my hand. Over fifteen years ago I had felt an electrical charge I could not explain pass through our bodies—something powerful, healing, a kind of grace emanated out of his hands. I trusted what was happening. I let go of the urge to control, the neediness. I allowed us to be together in this moment of possibilities.

We took a taxi home. I leaned forward from the back seat so my hips would be as high as possible. I walked to the front door of our community house with my hips jutted out in front, then climbed the ladder to our loft bed and propped pillows under my butt. I didn't dare go to the bathroom. I would lie back and imagine the bazillion sperm, setting off for Neverland, going up, up, up into the Milky Way. Each sperm helping the other, not leaving any behind, until they reached their destination and all turned to the special one, the future Alexander Spiro Burch, the one that would penetrate the egg. It was a eureka experience.

That night, I dreamt of a young girl. She was my child, our child, playing in the sand on the beach. I felt so much love for this little girl. I named her Anastasia, Sasha for short.

George teased, "fuchsia will be her favorite color."

"Are you really ready?" I asked.

"And if he is a boy, we'll call him Alexander," he said.

"No puns for Alex."

"I can't think of a single one," he said.

I dropped out of the support group the day after our insemination. I couldn't face another week of someone not getting pregnant. It felt like a support group for women on the edge of loosing their dreams. I wanted to be the first to skate on the crystal smooth ice rink, like when I was ten years old. I was going to spin and spin, like DNA, two strands intertwined, a blueprint for a new life.

Seven days after the insemination, I purchased the pregnancy kits and peed on the plastic sticks. No, not this time. I waited another day … it still seemed like we needed immaculate conception for the stick to show positive … no, the cross showed only a single line. I needed two lines to show through the tiny cardboard window. One more day, again no. At $20 a test, it was expensive, and I was losing heart. But I would try each day, eager to see the results.

On the fourth day of testing, I stared at the line, no lines, then two crossing lines emerged. I was pregnant! I dressed this pink plastic pregnancy test I had peed on with ribbons, wrapped it in pink tissue paper, bought helium balloons, and presented the trophy to George when he came home from work.

George and I celebrated, went out to dinner, talked about names again. George was beaming. We had fought this battle together. We were given a reprieve, a onetime success, and all because of George's healing. There was no other way to explain it—except perhaps George was ready to be a father now and nature supported his certainty. All his sperm tests had been so dismal, indicating that it was impossible to conceive under normal circumstances. We had experienced a phenomenon. Something neither medicine nor science could explain. A Divine intervention.

CHAPTER 3

REBIRTH

"My heart has been rent and joined again."

~ Hazrat Inayat Khan

The Penington Friends House, the brownstone in the East Village, was our home. Its motto was: a little peace of Manhattan. George and I lived in this small community of thirty people managed by Samantha, a dark-haired, vivacious woman, and David, her tall husband, a carpenter and painter. They had a six-year-old son and baby daughter. The family lived in the manager's apartment, which could be entered through a narrow office, where I worked on the bookkeeping, on the second floor.

The Penington had been set up nearly a hundred years previously by Quakers as a residence for people dedicated to making valuable contributions toward world peace, our planet, and each other. Most of us were not Quakers. Some of us worked in social services, but all of us wanted to live in community. George and I were the only married couple, besides the managers. We lived in one bedroom on the third floor. George's Greek Orthodox icon of St. George slaying the dragon was painted by his grandfather and hung on our bedroom wall. We had two closets, a mahogany framed mirror fastened over the marble mantel of a non-working fireplace, our loft bed, and bookshelves. Tight quarters.

To compensate for this matchbox space, the Penington had a double parlor on the second floor with two immense oriental rugs, a Victorian couch, a grandfather clock, wingback chairs, two chandeliers, and a fireplace, all in pretty good condition. Wolfie, my mother's African grey parrot, whom I had inherited, lived in a large brass cage in the living room.

Each time I walked through the iron gate, climbed the brownstone staircase, opened the heavy double glazed door, and entered the vestibule, I inhaled oxygen, fortified by the presence of peace, love, and care that infiltrated the walls, the rooms, and my body. I loved the Penington.

The place was always warm. George and I cracked the window in the middle of winter when the radiator drums began beating their warmth through our bedroom. My friend Marguerite shopped and cooked for all of us residents—going to the Union Street Greenmarket where she would find what was in season locally. She ordered organic grains in bulk before Whole Foods was in every major city. She poured a mixture of her Jewish love and herbs and spices from around the world into our dinners. Her own special blend of essence, a reverence for the gifts from the land, and the creativity of an artist inspired her meals that filled our stomachs, opened our hearts, and satisfied our souls. The aroma of Marguerite's Brunswick stew of cut-up chicken, homemade stock, lima beans, corn, tomatoes, clove, paprika, and thyme wafted up the stairs from the ground floor, where she cooked in an industrial size kitchen, calling me like a siren for my favorite dinner.

Dinners were bold events. Generation X twentysomethings, arrived from their colleges, dropped their bags, served themselves buffet style, and sat down at the long, narrow pinewood table in the dining room on the ground floor. Mary, an architecture student at Cooper Union, complained about her professor's unfair grade. Her boyfriend from Texas had a paper due the next day and hadn't even started the research. Then, there was the actress who went to daily auditions and supported herself by teaching tennis. We also had a middle-aged social worker who came home exhausted from all her clients she helped that day.

Emily was our middle-aged librarian who dyed her hair blond and converted to Judaism. She had raised a daughter, and now she was semi-retired. She was never pleased and always found something to complain about, the coffee was too bitter, the milk had been left out of the fridge, and there was no toilet paper in the bathroom again! But she was generous with her time and skills. She edited my film grant proposals, taught me to write, shook her head at my sloppy way of forgetting commas or putting them somewhere bizarre. She was a good friend.

Everyone tried to be home for dinner.

* * *

George loved the community, too. It reminded him of his Pyrgos village, where everyone knew each other. Greek men sat under the large oak tree sipping coffee and catching up on what happened overnight. George's great-grandfather imported fine merchandise from the Far East and other parts of Europe for the biggest store in the village, which he owned. The town was built high up on a mountain so that pirates could not see the village from the Mediterranean Sea.

The houses were set along narrow, winding roads, wide enough for mules and narrow enough that the black slate roofs touched each other. If the pirates did find the village, the villagers could run away on the rooftops further into the hills. Inside the house you could hear every word next door as if you were in the same room. George's soft-spoken voice, the same as his father's, was melodious and, I believed, a result of his family's heritage. My family was loud, argumentative, and quick to erupt into boisterous conflicts. If we had lived in Tinos, the whole village would have known our business.

* * *

At our community dinner, Emily worried about miscarriages during my first trimester. She told me to take it easy and not work so hard.

"Twenty percent of miscarriages happen during this time," she said.

"Don't worry. I'm not going anywhere, I'm having a blast," I said.

My skinny-for-me figure rounded out. I loved the change, imagining the cells dividing and dividing again. The fetus had been growing from a tadpole, to a bird like-creature, then to a tiny baby with miniscule fingers and toes. During the ultrasound, we saw a boy fetus, recognizable by his toothpick-size penis, swimming in green fluid. The fluttering feeling I had in my womb when he was in his chickie-like stage was gone, and now he kicked me with his two strong legs.

Three months later, I showed the ultrasound to my friends at another Penington dinner.

"I'm six months pregnant," I announced. Emily hugged me.

My friends at the Penington followed my progress, checked in regularly, and cared about my pregnancy. My own family took it for granted that all would be fine. They would get filled in at the next Thanksgiving, Easter, or Christmas dinner.

* * *

My grandmother, the only living relative I knew on my mother's side, lived on the opposite coast. My sister and I followed her recovery from her recent hospitalization long distance but with daily check-ins. We were her caretakers and closest family members after my mother died. My grandmother's social worker called and said my grandmother was not sleeping. She had been pacing in her living room for two nights. My grandmother's live-in aide was at her wits' end. I booked a flight for the next day for San Francisco.

On the five-hour flight, I felt guilty that I hadn't visited my grandmother after she was hospitalized. I didn't want to take any risks by flying in my first trimester. Elena, my sister, had just had her first child and couldn't travel either.

Five months previously, the neighbors had found my

grandmother collapsed in her home. The emergency room doctor diagnosed a problem with her heart, but then another set of doctors operated on her intestines for diverticulitis, inflammation of the inner lining of the intestine and colon. Her primary physician thought the cause of her collapse was dehydration, a common condition in the elderly. The final diagnosis on discharge was congestive heart failure, a buildup of fluid in the lungs, and she went home with multiple prescriptions.

After my grandmother was released from the hospital, she was still quite sick. Elena and I handled our grandmother's crisis together from afar. We hired a social worker, health care aides, and set up full-service, 24-hour care in her home. My grandmother loved San Francisco and her grey long-haired Himalayan cat, Baby Love. She had made it clear that she and her cat wanted to live the rest of their days in her home in Pacific Heights. She had the money to afford it.

My grandmother had been independent and living on her own for two years after her second husband died. She was financially smart, worked as a government federal secretary for the pension benefit, and for the Blue Cross Blue Shield insurance, promising the best healthcare coverage (so she told me). She had invested wisely the pay-out from my grandfather's death insurance, and lived frugally—although with an air of wealth that came from recognizing the best and finding it at the next-to-new shops. Pewter was her passion. She could point to some blackened old object on a far dusty shelf in an antique store. And, after lengthy bargaining with the owner, he would agree to sell the object to her for $20. And when my grandmother presented her Certified Interior Decorator card that guaranteed her another 15% off, the exasperated storekeeper would give up and hand over the valuable object. Back home, my grandmother cleaned her new treasure, checked its stamps (indicating its maker or time period) on the bottom of the object, and most times she ended up with a precious English pewter piece. She documented on index cards every antique she owned for insurance purposes and proved their value based on her extensive research. She was called by the Getty Museum at times to help identify pewter pieces in their collection.

At the airport, I took the Super Shuttle to my grandmother's apartment. I had visited rarely because she was estranged from my mother. The last time I had come was to help when her second husband, Freddy, had several strokes and could no longer care for himself. We moved him into a nursing home, a full-care facility, but his stay was short. He refused to eat and starved himself to death.

The fog horns moaned outside my grandmother's sixth floor apartment on Jackson Street. The stone apartment building, built after the 1906 earthquake, had a solid, immovable, and fortified foundation. My grandmother had lived there for over fifty years. Her living room looked like a spread from Architectural Digest. The sheepskin white rug, the large German and English pewter platters from the Middle Ages, a 17th century Japanese gold painted screen of evergreens, and a Louis XIV mantel clock were boldly exhibited in the double living room with two marble mantel fireplaces, facing each other at the far end of the rooms.

I found her dressed in a rose-colored quilted robe and pacing around her plush white living room, repeating, "Where am I? Where am I? Where? Am? I?" The aide, exhausted, had gone home as soon as I arrived. She had explained that this was now her fourth night without sleep.

The elegant grandmother of my memory now appeared disheveled, her white hair standing up in all direction. Her lips pursed and not painted. Her eyes darted from one corner of the room to another, not focusing on anything in particular. I sat on her white settee, where she used to play solitaire on a wooden breakfast tray.

My grandmother had told me that she had fallen in love with San Francisco the first time she laid eyes on it. She had arrived by ferryboat, alone, on a foggy evening in February. She said the diffused street lamps revealed none of the city's beauty until the next day when the sun shone and the blue skies painted a stunning background behind the rolling hills and Victorian homes. This city was a new beginning for her as a young widow. After the tragic death of her husband in a drunk driving accident, she had left her young daughter, my mother, with her mother in North Carolina to start a new chapter. She bought the apartment she now lived in by selling the telluride mineral rights she inherited from her deceased husband.

"Where am I?" my grandmother repeated again in her raspy voice, her clever, witty mind devastated by the illness. On the coffee table were ten orange plastic medicine bottles with white labels and typed prescriptions.

I plugged in my 18-pound Toshiba with its orange screen and opened the document with a list of my grandmother's medications that I had created. I reviewed the records: antidepressants, stimulants, antipsychotic drugs, and new SSRIs, a cocktail of drugs for mood disorders; modern beta blockers, ancient digitalis preparations, and common diuretics for the congestive heart failure.

At nine p.m., midnight for me, I stopped all the psychiatric medications. Cold turkey. For two more hours my grandmother circled the living room. A new moaning sound began alternating with her mantra, "Where am I?" Then she stopped moving forward, and started to sway right and left. She looked at me for the first time.

"I'm tired. Can I sleep now?" she asked, making eye contact.

I hugged my grandmother for the first time since I arrived. She leaned into me, her petite, four-foot ten-inch frame, wrapped over my protruding belly. Arm in arm, we walked to her bedroom, decorated in champagne pink and rustic green. I tucked her under her peach-colored satin covers in her antique French latticework bed. She breathed normally and fell asleep almost immediately.

When I awoke the next morning, my grandmother was still asleep. It wasn't until noon when she came out, dressed in rust wool slacks, an ivory turtleneck, and her large amber necklace dangling on her chest.

"Good morning," she said.

"More like good afternoon," I said.

She chuckled.

"When did you arrive?" she asked.

"I was here last night."

"Really? You must have gotten here after I went to bed. Sorry I wasn't here to welcome you."

She really had no memory of the last four days.

"And here you're pregnant. It's so lovely you came to visit me," she smiled at my big belly.

I called her general practitioner and left a message. When the doctor called back, I told her that I had discontinued all the psychiatric drugs and had only given my grandmother her heart medications. The doctor told me that a psychiatrist had prescribed the other drugs when my grandmother had been discharged from the hospital. I called that psychiatrist and told him what happened.

"I'm coming over to examine your grandmother," Dr. Manfield told me.

In less than an hour he rang the doorbell, and I escorted him up the narrow steps into the living room where my grandmother was sitting on her settee, playing cards and drinking black coffee. Her empty ashtray was on the side table, left there from the time when she smoked three packs of Kent Lights a day. She had told me she quit smoking at the hospital and wasn't going to start up again. And she seemed to mean it.

Dr. Manfield, tall, wearing an elegant grey suit and silver-framed spectacles perched on the tip of his nose, pulled up a chair next to my grandmother.

"What date is today?" he asked.

"It's Tuesday, February 17th," my grandmother replied.

"Who is the president?"

"Bill Clinton," she answered correctly.

"What did you have for breakfast Mrs. Robinson?"

"Oh, just coffee—taking care of my figure you know," she giggled.

My grandmother loved to flirt with younger men, which meant pretty much any man she met. She was ninety years old, still batted her lashes, and spoke with a Bette Davis voice when she wanted to be seductive.

After the mad woman I saw last night, I couldn't imagine a happier elderly lady. Dr. Manfield, forty-something, smiled at my grandmother.

"You must call me Eunice," she said.

"Eunice?"

"A man like you must be quite the catch among the nurses," she said.

They were getting along famously. The doctor accepted my offer of coffee and made himself comfortable.

"You're fit as a fiddle, and I'm happy to see you doing so well in your own home," he said.

I couldn't have agreed more. Then I showed him out, walking down the long staircase to the entrance which led to the stone steps outside, six flights down to Jackson Street. My grandmother had easily gone up and down those stairs for half a century, carrying groceries, her next-to-new purchases of designer clothes, and antiques.

Dr. Manfield turned to me on the landing outside and said, "We will have to commit your grandmother for her own safety."

"What?" I couldn't believe what I'd heard.

"She must be in full psychiatric care in a hospital," he said. "It's best for her."

"This makes no sense, she's fine. You told her yourself how pleased you are with her health. Why are you recommending she goes to a hospital now?" I asked.

"You've been reckless, stopping her medications and against all medical advice."

What a stone-faced, deceitful man! I couldn't believe he had taken a Hippocratic oath. He was the one who had been reckless, prescribing all those useless drugs that had made her crazy.

I made up my mind right then and there to take her home to live with George, our future baby, and myself in New York at the Penington Friends House.

"You're going against medical advice," were the doctor's final words.

* * *

I'd heard those same words just a week earlier. I was walking down the hall of the Roosevelt Hospital after a routine blood test ordered by my midwives, when a short, stocky doctor in a white coat stopped me by the elevator. I had never met him before.

"It's flu season. You must be vaccinated right away," the doctor said, looking at my belly.

I recoiled from the suggestion. My maternal instincts kicked in. I felt complete repulsion to the idea.

"What? I need time to research this … never heard of flu vaccinations required," I stammered, sure I hadn't missed anything in my research on the internet or in the book, *What to Expect When You're Expecting*. Something in me knew he was wrong.

"Your baby will be deformed or worse, if you don't get this flu vaccination," he said.

"Are you saying this may happen if I get the flu while I'm pregnant?" I asked, caught off guard.

"This is a serious choice. May I remind you that not getting vaccinated is going against medical advice," he said. "I'll have to report this disobedience in your medical records."

"OK, do what you have to do, but I'm not getting a flu shot," I stormed out, shaking. He never told me his name.

* * *

My grandmother fit right into the Penington. She moved into the guest room with Baby Love, her cat. She would sit at the center of the long dining table and tell stories about her childhood.

"One time I was so mad at my older brother—who got all of my mother's attention—that I thought, what is the worst thing I could do to him? So I went to the penny store and bought the cheapest, most awful smelling perfume and poured it on his pillow. Of course, my mother made me wash the pillow case over and over to get rid of the smell."

My grandmother smiled her girlish smile then looked over at Paul, a man fifteen years younger than her, who wore his pants high over his big belly with yellow suspenders. She had his rapt attention.

Later, Paul and my grandmother became an item. They were quite a pair. He couldn't see and she could barely hear. Arm in arm, they strolled the streets of Manhattan like young lovers.

When my grandmother came to live with us, George made a living by keeping up with all of his part-time jobs. He continued to attend his energy healing school that I believed helped me become pregnant. He was like Pan, the Greek god, running from one interest to the next, discovering himself, making himself useful wherever he could. My grandmother loved him.

While I was pregnant, I kept my full-time secretary position at Dillon Read. My routine didn't change much as Alex grew in my belly. I meditated under the loft bed every morning on a chair. I read spiritual and self-help books like Don Miguel Angel Ruiz's *The Four Agreements: A Practical Guide to Personal Freedom*. My inner core, broken and mended so many times, impelled me to seek out better tools than what I had learned from my parents. These books were my personal development training to prepare me for this next stage of life as a mother.

George read his occult books, mostly channeled sources about creation, entities, and spirits like *Emmanuel's Book II: The Choice for Love*, written by Pat Rodegast. We shared spirituality, a knowingness that there was spirit and something more to life than just a material world, but we had different ways of practice. And the arrangement at the Penington left us plenty of time to pursue our passions.

* * *

I was in constant motion as another trimester passed. Life moved at a fast pace, in the midst of community, sharing meals together, watching movies, doing our chores, working. I observed myself, based on my Gurdjieff practice, which I had studied in my 20s. I saw how each person had their own rationale for their actions; there was not only one way to be or to think. The diversity of living with a variety of people proved to be a learning ground for compassion and growth.

I was also shooting and editing the national public television series, *Women in Limbo Presents*, about women's lives. At Women in Limbo, I filmed women from multiracial and different economic backgrounds standing on a small stage in the Knitting Factory, sharing their personal stories week after week on themes like mothers and daughters, money, self-esteem.

My partner, Sarah, and I were creating a national public television series which showed how we each had our own way—nothing was all that unique, either. We were all humans who shared common values, solutions, and struggles, too. Exhilarated by the life I had composed; I saw in each woman's story a heroic journey. We were strong, cutting-edge, vocal, and inspiring. The creative and spiritual parts of me had been lived separately, but I started to connect them as an integrated way of life. My identity was being redefined. Instead of meditating in a cave, could I be a mother, a whole person, a healer, aware in the moment during daily life?

I was also the lover. George and I were building our life together while supporting each other's independence. I was thirty-five and time was moving fast. I had few attachments—until Alex arrived.

* * *

"What does your baby want to say to you?" asked the yoga teacher, at the end of the two-hour prenatal yoga class.

Now four days overdue, and on maternity leave from my assistant job at Dillon Read that paid well and a boss who expected no real work, I was enjoying these last days of pregnancy.

"I want out," I heard as clear as day.

On my walk home from class, there were the first twinges of sharp pains coming at regular fifteen-minute intervals. I breathed through the contractions, as I made my way to our new one-bedroom apartment, six blocks from the Penington, where we moved to have more space for our growing family. At the Penington, my grandmother had moved into our old room with Baby Love. I called Alana, our doula and labor coach, who advised me to take it easy. I called our midwives, and the midwife on duty told us to keep in touch. I called George and told him what was happening, but there was no urgency yet.

By 10 p.m., the cramps were eight minutes apart and lasting a minute and half. George was exhausted from guiding me through the long, deep breaths. They were based on the Bradley method we learned at the classes—the opposite of the hyperventilating breathing method taught at Lamaze classes.

Alana arrived at 1 a.m. to relieve George, who could finally take a nap. She had left three children sleeping with her husband. My contractions slowed down—back to 10 minutes apart, 15 minutes apart, even 20 minutes. I felt guilty keeping Alana up through the night when she was no longer needed. She didn't mind and kept me company. We sat on cushions on the living room floor. She held my hands as each contraction came, one less and less intense than before and further apart.

When the sun came up, I was starving. We ordered hamburgers and French fries and ate with relish. I felt fantastic, rested without any sleep, calm, and confident. We visited the Penington where our friends greeted us. My grandmother had not slept all night in anticipation of the arrival her great-grandson. I was on a high.

"Please give Melissa back her labor," Alana teased my grandmother, as we sat in the backyard.

We laughed under the tall city trees, beside the pink impatiens planted in the garden. A family pod, George, my grandmother, me, and our helpers supported by the Penington, a little peace of Manhattan.

Alana left to call the midwife, who was not pleased with the situation.

"Your midwife on call wants you to go to your apartment immediately, take four ounces of castor oil, and come to the hospital after your labor is back on track," Alana said, when she returned from the phone call.

The thought of drinking castor oil made me nauseous. I had read how sick it could make a pregnant woman—first explosive diarrhea and then stomach cramps. No thank you.

"You're having too much fun," Alana said. "We need a conference."

"I can stimulate my nipples—I know this brings on volcanic contractions. I hadn't said anything before because they were so painful when I tried it before you came," I said.

"OK, we must follow her orders, but you can do the nipple stimulations while we walk back to your apartment," Alana said. We had a plan.

On the third nipple massage, eruptive contractions exploded on 17th street near Gramercy Park. A big splash gushed between my legs, drenching the bottom half of my purple cotton dress. My sandals turned squishy. Four blocks to go and contractions were coming every minute, lasting over a minute; the walk took an hour and ten minutes. I was laboring on the streets of Manhattan held by George and small but strong Alana. When we arrived in the apartment, I was in full labor. Alana supported me into the shower. She placed a few pellets of a homeopathic remedy in my mouth; I tasted the sweet pellets, and my labor went into hyperdrive. George grabbed my overnight bag, which had been packed for this event over a week ago. Hanging on to George, we went to Alana's car.

"Nobody noticed anything; it's New York," I whispered to George during the short break between the painful contractions.

"They noticed," George said.

I tried to time the contraction so it wouldn't happen in front of our doorman. Alana's green station wagon was idling for us. I twisted, turned, moaned, and wailed, as I climbed into the back seat on my knees and hung over the cargo back. We crossed town from 2nd Avenue to 10th Avenue to 59th street to Roosevelt Hospital's birthing center. We arrived at the hospital; I had one contraction at the main entrance, one in the elevator, and one at the door of the birthing center. Sandy, the on-call midwife, greeted me and brought us into our private room.

"Please lie on your back," Sandy requested.

"I can't do it. I can't do it," I said.

"Yes, you can. Yes, you can," she said in a kind but firm tone.

I was on my back.

"She's 9 ½ cm, the head is showing," Sandy said.

Oh my God, I had made it through transition. My greatest fear was that I wouldn't make it through the last part of labor without screaming for an epidural, but I'd passed through that hurdle. Sandy asked me to lie on my side to push this baby out.

"I'm going to squat. I'm an excellent squatter. I'm strong and ready to squat," I said with a conviction I had developed after watching a documentary about African bush women who gave birth easily in a squat position.

"Nope," Sandy said. "You're going to lie on your side."

I laid on my side, but I felt I was on top of a mountain. I was a lioness roaring as loudly and as ferociously as I could. I was in this primal labor, birthing a new me, as I bore my son. I pushed strongly. I was the mountain lioness. Alex's head popped out.

"Do you want to see him?" Sandy asked, holding a mirror.

"NO!" I roared, pushed, and felt the rest of his body plopping out of me.

In an instant, Alex was in my arms. George held back tears, as he cradled both of us. He was wearing his "IM Love" T-shirt from his energy healing school. Alex looked around at George and me. He looked so perfect, not crunchy pink, a beautiful boy, with a round head, dark-haired, skin so soft, not bloody. This baby felt big and heavy in my arms. He was here with us.

"You look so beautiful. You'll meet your great-grandmother soon. You're so adorable," I cooed.

Mild contractions followed, and the placenta was expelled.

"Do you want the placenta?" Sandy asked.

"No, thank you," I said. Alana wanted it for fertilizer for her garden. George cut Alex's umbilical cord. Then George stared into my eyes; calm, grace, and warmth permeated me.

"Paps Mou, I adore you," I said.

Alana and Sandy supported us; never once did I feel anxious, panicked, or fearful. Hours after Alex's birth, we refused the Hepatitis A vaccination for sexually transmitted disease, but we were forced to accept the silver nitrate eye drops to prevent blindness—in case I had gonorrhea, which I did not have. No way to go against this medical advice.

We also chose not to circumcise Alex, as part of our natural birth plan. And circumcision was not an acceptable practice in the Greek Orthodox community.

Alexander Spiro Burch yawned, and the midwife guided my nipple into his wide open mouth. Within seconds, he was sucking my breast. We were united again.

A glowing light filled the room. The time of birth was 12:50 p.m. on Tuesday, July 1st, 1997. I was a mother, George was a father, we were parents of a healthy Cancer boy.

The next morning, my father arrived in his brand new green Bentley. We ordered bagels, cream cheese, and lox from a local Greek diner. We enjoyed breakfast together in the birthing center room, which looked more like a Marriott hotel room than any hospital I had ever visited. There was a walk-in Jacuzzi we never had the chance to use, matching floral curtains and bedspread, and a round glass dining table.

Two days later, we celebrated the Fourth of July on the roof of the Penington with my grandmother, her boyfriend Paul, and all our friends. Alex slept in my arms, as bursts of light erupted over the sky and loud explosions followed.

CHAPTER 4

BLESSINGS

"My heart has been broken and again made whole."

~ Hazrat Inayat Khan

In the center of the Tinos village, an ancient oak tree, at least ten generations old, provided shade, a refuge from daily life. It had witnessed all of George's family's rites of passage—baptisms, weddings, and funerals—for generations. *Cafenions*, tavernas, and the public water fountain surrounded this deep-rooted tree. After Alex's Greek Orthodox baptism, George and I served over a hundred individual chocolate cakes with the name Spiro handwritten on them to our two families, guests, villagers, and tourists under the tree's canopy. Alex had fallen asleep and was resting in a sling across my chest, oblivious to all the well-wishers. "*Na sas zisi.*" May he live for you.

George's father, Spiro, forgave us when his community of Pyrgos' villagers repeated Spiro, the baby's name, over and over, and pointed at his name-cakes, smiling. We had broken tradition by giving him my last name, Burch, but also by giving out cakes instead of the usual foil-wrapped chocolates.

My father, the patriarch of my family, celebrated with Spiro, the patriarch of George's family. My father identified with his own tobacco growing, North Carolinian relatives, who enjoyed hanging out on porches and telling stories with family and neighbors in similar ways to the mostly merchant marine families living on Tinos. My father, who had become a Zen Buddhist, felt a resonance with the Greek Orthodox baptismal chanting with its symbolisms of water, oil, and fire. He greeted each person with a short bow, in the Zen tradition.

My trauma, after the wrestling match in the church, was all my own. George seemed resigned to what had happened. I wanted something different, a celebration of our new family, this new soul that we would shepherd until he could care for himself.

"George, how about we do our own baptism? We could find one of those sacred places on the cliffs of Tinos, you know the ones where mystical women come to enchant the men, steal them for a night of pleasure," I was teasing George a bit. Island folklore had stories of *xotika*, female spirits kidnapping men for a sexual orgy if they went to the *alonias*, the threshing floors, on a full moon night.

"You mean the *alonia* where the wheat was chaffed in the old days," he said.

"Yes, I want us to create a ritual that blesses Alex, gives him wishes we want him to have, based on our values. This church experience was too much focused on evil and belonging to Christ," I said.

"Something more universal and spiritual?" George asked.

"Yes."

The day after his baptism Alex slept more than 16 hours. I almost woke him up, worried that he was ill, but I let him sleep. I could see he was breathing. We drove the white rental jeep, our nuclear family looking for the spot where we could see the sun rise over the Mediterranean sea. Before Alex came to us, George and I had toured most of the island, me riding behind George holding on to him, as he drove the motorbike. Now, we were looking for *alonia*, the most beautiful threshing circle we had discovered on our explorations.

This baptism would be a private affair. George and I had planned it ourselves, too self-conscious to open the ritual to relatives and friends. My father's Buddhist tradition wasn't mine. I didn't want any Christian influences. We were on our own to imagine something different.

We set the date for September 3rd, 1997 at sunrise. We packed a backpack with a candle, water, incense, and a crystal, representing the four elements: water, air, fire, and earth. We wrote our blessings and planned to recite them in the four directions, east, south, west, and north, as we honored Alex.

The night before, we tried to sleep in the fold-out couch in the tiny stucco house that George's father's grandparents had built: three-feet stone walls with a simple kitchen, bathroom, and one living room. The two windows with their Greek blue shutters faced the sea.

That night, the winds howled and the shutters banged. The chairs on the terrace were thrown down, making crashing sounds and scraping noises as the wind pushed them across the walled-in area. Rain pelted down on the slate roof. During August and early September, winds could be strong but a rainstorm was unusual. All night, the banging kept George and me awake. Alex woke every two hours for his breast feeding, undisturbed by the commotion outside.

"Do you think this weather is an omen?" George asked.

"Bad spirits warning us not to tamper with things," I said.

"Yes, it might be wrong for us to make our own ceremony. It feels like we're not meant to do the service we planned."

"It couldn't be any worse than what Alex has been through already with the Greek Orthodox Church," I said.

"No, this is different. I don't feel it's right. We need to call it off."

I felt something too, not sure what it meant, but maybe this event should not happen at this time.

"Let's see what happens, OK?" I said.

The next day we didn't go to the alonia. In the evening, a glorious sunset reigned over the island which felt washed, cleansed, and transformed after the previous night's rainstorm.

The alarm went off on September 4th. It was dark outside, the moon had set hours before, and the stars shone bright but distant. I wore Alex around my chest in the baby sling, and George swung the backpack with our tools and sacred objects on his shoulder. All the marble paved paths were empty, the tavernas facing the sea were closed. The sea lapped on the shore near where our jeep was parked. Alex relaxed in my arms and slept as we drove to our magical spot.

The sound of the car motor, the fresh sea breeze, George clasped my hand as he drove—we were cocooned in our bond as a family. My heart opened in this metal carriage, as we climbed the Tinos hills, winding up higher and higher on the dirt road. George parked the car on the side of the road. Alex woke up and nursed, while George set up the ritual. He took out of his backpack the candle, water bottle, crystal, and incense and placed them on the wall that surrounded the miniature amphitheater-like space where we would invoke Spirit to support our child on this earth.

George and I faced the sun, a ball of fire, as it rose from the sea. We sang "Our Baby Is so Fine," a song I'd made up weeks before in the singing class that helped me conquer my fear of singing out loud. I had been ashamed of my croaking voice and inability to carry a tune. I wanted to be able to sing lullabies to my baby. It took all my courage to sing the graduating song by myself on the last day of class.

Now, I felt at ease, as George and I sang our song to our son, "Our Baby Is so Fine," a one-line tune, over and over. The sun cast a golden light over us. George poured the water over the crystal in the center of the alonia, facing east, and prayed.

"Look into ourselves and be a part of all that exists," we said in unison.

Then I lit the candle, cupping the flame with my hand to keep it alight, and faced south.

"We want to be reminded of the beauty and love that surrounds us, the wholeness and divinity that resides in each of us," we said.

Then George lit the incense, twirls of smoke spiraled up to the sky. We faced west.

"May we be of service in our work, in our family and friendships, and be aware of all creatures and their way of being."

Then we turned north, and I took the crystal, a clear obelisk-shaped quartz rock, and placed it in front of us.

"For Alexander Spiro Burch, we wish you a healthy and strong body and a passionate, full of love, prosperous, gentle, patient, fulfilling, compassionate, giving, caring, long, and joyous existence. We celebrate your beautiful soul. We love you, Alexander," George and I hugged our son in my arms.

That night, the white, thin, cotton curtains billowed over our bed. Alex slept soundly next to us on a tiny bed pushed up against our queen-sized bed. The stars birthed more stars that night. Shooting stars jetted across the night sky. In a sea of desire, George entered me and pulled me into a sense of oneness, where I became those stars, breathed the galaxies—human and celestial combined in timeless lovemaking.

SECOND PART
SYNCHRONICITIES

"My heart has been wounded and healed again."

~ Hazrat Inayat Khan

CHAPTER 5
MAGIC

"A thousand deaths my heart has died, and thanks be to love, it lives yet."

~ Hazrat Inayat Khan

On the Tuesday after Labor Day, a whiff of a fall breeze cooled the soon-to-be hot day. I pushed Alex uptown on 3rd Avenue in his new blue Maclaren stroller, a baby shower gift from my coworkers at Dillon Read. We were heading to the ATM cubicle in the middle of the block between 18th and 19th Streets. I was jetlagged from the return flight from Greece. The yellow taxis, city buses, and cars whirled past us going downtown during the morning rush hour traffic.

It was the first time since I was a teenager that I was not working, checking off a to-do list, or planning years in advance. Before Alex was born, George and I figured I would go back to work full-time and Alex would be dropped off at daycare each morning. But when I held Alex moments after his birth, I knew nobody but me would care for this child during the week.

His old man-like face—an I've-been-here-before and a-whole lifetime-to-do-over expression on his face—radiated from his dark brown eyes. My job would be to keep him alive and nourished.

George's hodgepodge of jobs hardly paid for the rental, nor

all the additional expenses of an expanded family. But with our newfound freedom, we had charged our credit cards and gone to Greece for the baptism anyway. Now back home, I was going to take out the last $100 from the bank.

In the glass walled mini-bank, Alex, dressed in his baby jean overalls and Gap t-shirt, watched the back of my thighs. His view of our city outings would be two feet off the ground for the next months, until he could walk. I shoved my plastic bankcard into the metal machine, punched in the four-digit passcode, and looked at the balance. $2,197 flickered on the screen.

"WOW!" I said out loud.

What was going on? There must be an error. This was impossible. The only explanation I could think of was that Dillon Read had not processed my resignation. They thought I was still working there.

Alex and I returned to our apartment on 21st Street and took the elevator to the tenth floor. It had felt like a million miles when I was in labor, but now in less than a minute we arrived to our floor. I grabbed the unopened pile of mail from the table and found the bank statement. There were four deposits, the exact amount of my weekly paycheck from Dillon Read. I was grateful.

Do babies come into the world with a line of credit? I planned to pay the company back as soon as we could afford to. Grace had helped us at this time of need.

* * *

On Sunday, George and I read *The New York Times* employment section. I circled every possible tech job in red ink. George applied to all of the jobs. He was going to be the breadwinner, the stereotypical father and husband, while I stayed home to be the mother and wife. I insisted he find a full-time, well-paying job with health insurance, something I could not live without now that we had a child. In a few weeks, he got a job at the American Civil Liberties Union as a PC specialist, his first full-time corporate job with benefits.

The hormones rushing through my body pumped me up so much I was thinking about having a second child. I loved the minutiae of life, eating to produce milk, breastfeeding, changing diapers. George and I enjoyed our evenings together when he came home from work: almost a *Father Knows Best* TV scene, except Marguerite cooked our meals. George, Alex in his stroller, and I walked to the Penington for community dinners shared with my grandmother and our friends. My feminist self was dislodged by this ancient role of motherhood. All-consumed by this female stereotype, I felt good and at ease.

Mesimerianos ipnos, siestas—Alex and I curled up together on the bed, following each other's rhythms—were part of daily life. Since Alex didn't seem to require much sleep, even for a newborn, I took advantage of all of his naps to catch up on my broken sleep. Most of the time, I fell asleep when he did. My years of workaholic tendencies were being remedied.

* * *

Dillon Read deposited a second month of payroll and an additional $4,000. I called them to find out what was happening. Swiss Bank had bought Dillon Read while we were in Greece. Retroactively, I had been reinstated with six months full-pay, European child leave benefits (instead of the typical six weeks in the U.S.). Since the takeover, they also gave me a severance package because they were moving the company to Connecticut. A Christmas bonus was also deposited into my bank account. Over $20,000 appeared over the course of the year, including state unemployment benefits, and a small business grant I qualified for during this time.

Who would have known? I trusted my instincts and was more than rewarded for doing what felt right. I had tested my intuition in extreme situations in Afghanistan, when I had had the courage in a war zone to act on an absurd notion that ended up saving my life and the lives of the mujahedeen I had been embedded with. Since my twenties, I had followed my gut. This way of life had become second nature for me as a new mother.

Sometimes I kept having the same thought over and over. I must do something that felt exciting and fearful, like rappelling off a cliff—most often this idea worked out for the best. If I had a repetitive thought that felt icky or drained energy or a sickly terror like a mugger approaching, then I knew that acting on it would be a wrong course of action and would quickly go in a different direction. And I checked intuition against common sense. Intuition without common sense was stupidity.

* * *

On an afternoon when I would normally sleep with Alex, I had an idea. I sat on the oversized green couch in our 150 square-foot living room, dining room, and kitchen with one window that faced a brick wall, the yellow pages on my lap opened to homeopaths. Alex was sound asleep, snuggled into his bassinet on the floor. There were six listings; only one had the letters MD next to the name. I pushed the numbers on the corded phone of the first name.

"Hi, this is Melissa Burch. I'm a new mother. I have a question about vaccinations. Can you please call me back? Thank you," I left the message on the voice mail.

I repeated this message four more times. Then, I heard the familiar click—one of the homeopaths was calling me back. I answered.

"This is Philip Seymour returning your call," the homeopath said.

"Great, I think I'm looking for a home-opp-pi-thist …"

"I'm a homeopath."

"Can you tell me how long you've been in practice?" That was the first question recommended in the pamphlet, "How To Choose a Pediatrician."

"Huh, I don't know. A few years?" he said.

"Where did you train?"

"Mostly read books," he answered.

This conversation was not going well. I had expected that homeopaths were like doctors and would readily provide credentials that sounded plausible for their role as healers.

I hung up and called the MD homeopath. Dr. Buten answered the phone on the second ring. He told me he had been to Stanford

Medical School, studied homeopathy with George Vithoulkas on Alonissos in Greece, and treated babies. I made an appointment with him.

* * *

The most difficult decision George and I made was not to vaccinate Alex at birth. We did not think he was at risk for Hepatitis B, a sexually transmitted disease. But now I was researching the vaccination question and discovered there was a lot of controversy. The Centers for Disease Control, the American Medical Association, and the American Pediatric Society were unanimous: Vaccinations saved lives. No debate. As parents, we were questioning some of the current popular childrearing ideas. Alex slept with us in a crib pushed up and attached to our bed (an adapted family bed), which was frowned on by many experts. I put Alex on his stomach when he was fussy sleeping on his back. He was calm, safe, and content sleeping on his stomach.

However, the lonely voices of homeopaths were arguing against vaccinations. They countered this all-out war against diseases with articles and books. They spoke about the immune system and how getting some childhood diseases like measles made children stronger. I was thankful that I had measles as a child, one less worry of a risk for a miscarriage when I was pregnant. I wanted to find out what a homeopath would say about vaccinating Alex.

* * *

At a Park Avenue apartment building, a doorman told me I could enter Dr. Buten's office on the ground floor. There was no receptionist or waiting room. In a large, oak-paneled room, the doctor, a burly fellow, stood up and shook my hand across his desk. Alex was sitting in his stroller. I unfastened him and sat him on my lap.

"When was Alex born?" the doctor asked, as he began taking notes.

I told the doctor about the minor complaints. Alex woke up

every few hours in the night, didn't take long naps, and then my decision to postpone the vaccinations.

"According to the Homeopathic Medical Society of the State of New York charter, you must vaccinate your child," he told me.

"That's strange, I thought homeopaths were against vaccinations," I said.

"Not so," he said.

He was not open to discussing the issue. He did not examine Alex. He did not administer vaccinations. I would have to go to Alex's pediatrician for the recommended immunizations. He would not treat my son if he became ill.

"What?" I asked. "You said on the phone you treated babies."

"I give constitutional remedies only."

I had no idea what he was talking about.

"For acutes, I recommend you buy Dana Ullman's book, *Homeopathic Medicine for Children and Infants*, and a Boiron homeopathic kit of fifty remedies in 30c," he said.

"You mean I'm to treat my own child if he gets sick?"

"Yes."

"This is preposterous!" I said.

I looked over his shoulder at his framed medical license and medical school diploma. They looked authentic, but he was a quack. I was being scammed. His fee was $400 and was not covered by insurance. I put Alex back in his stroller. My hand shook with rage, as I wrote out the check.

I told George what had happened. He was the type to give everyone the benefit of the doubt. I wasn't so sure. But this vaccination and homeopathy question persisted in my mind.

* * *

I bought the book Dr. Buten recommended. I even bought the homeopathic kit. Ullman's book prescribed homeopathic remedies for common ailments: For example, take three pellets of Belladonna for high fever. Isn't Belladonna poisonous? In the book's reference, I found Dr. George Vithoulkas' book, *The Science of Homeopathy*, listed. Despite my skepticism, I was curious.

In Vithoulkas' book, I discovered that homeopathic remedies were so diluted, beyond Avogadro's number, that not a single molecule of the original substance could be in it. The remedies transmitted information that stimulated the vital force, the chi, to restore a person to health. Before going to the birthing center, the sweetness I tasted during labor had been the milk sugar pellets my doula popped into my mouth. The homeopathic remedy seemed benign at the time, but I was to discover the power of homeopathy.

Vithoulkas wrote about homeopathic laws—minimum dose, like cures like, direction of cure. I understood none of these concepts, but I was fascinated. This medical modality made no sense, but neither did energy healing, although Alex was the proof that there might be something to it. I was willing to explore the unknown. I would suspend judgment. George, far more experimental than I, enjoyed the information about homeopathy. He agreed with the tenet of homeopathy that less is better. The pediatrician would be in charge of Alex's medical care—but Dr. Buten's proclamation chipped at my certainty. Could there be a different way?

* * *

At four months old, Alex was a plump baby. I still had not vaccinated him. I was not sure what I was waiting for. Walking down Broadway in Soho, pushing Alex in his stroller, I turned left on Prince Street where the Open Center had an esoteric bookstore I loved to browse. On the bulletin board, there was a flyer for a homeopathic lecture by Harold Thompson on Friday night. I decided to go.

The cedar incensed room, dim lights, altar in the corner, and a new-age reverence at the Open Center meeting room greeted me as I sat down next to 20 other New Yorkers for Harold Thompson's lecture. With his rumpled grey suit, unshaven jaw, and Einstein-like hair, Harold did not fit in this setting. He asked for a chalkboard and pulled out of his pocket white chalk that smeared all over his suit. An assistant in tight yoga pants obliged him.

He drew a circle on the chalkboard.

"Think! This is the Sulphur remedy," he said. "Imagine a

messy person, full of ideas, itchy skin, sticks his feet out of bed to cool them, craves eggs."

I was sure he was talking about himself. He labeled the circle Sulphur. Then he drew another circle.

"Sulphur meets Sepia, a homeopathic remedy made from cuttlefish," he said. "The Sepia woman is independent, yells at her kids, wants to be left alone, has irregular menstruation, lacks vital heat, thirsty."

"What a pair these two would make?" I joked with the class.

My mind rushed with ideas about a universe where a medicine had personality—individualized prescriptions based on a cluster of characteristics, not symptoms or a diagnosis. I was still wrapping my brain around the idea that there was nothing in those sugar pellets. This sounded like magic.

While I listened to Harold, I found myself interested in studying medicine for the first time. George's energy healing dabbling had been the Holy Grail for us, after the canary in the coal mine experience with conventional medicine. The unexplainable had led us to getting pregnant and having a healthy baby boy, against all medical predictions. Was it possible that there was something to this homeopathy, too?

"The universe is interconnected, and homeopathy is a part of this paradigm," Harold said.

I was hooked. Spirituality and medicine combined. Not for an instant did I believe homeopathy could cure anything but I loved the ideas. I signed up for his three-month course.

* * *

For Thanksgiving, George drove our family, including my grandmother, to my father's house in Concord in our 1980s green Volvo. I sat up front. Alex was strapped in his car seat next to Baby Love, who was meowing in his plastic carrier.

"It's OK, we'll be there soon," my grandmother told her cat over and over.

We arrived as the brown roasted turkey was coming out of the oven. My father, his wife, their nine-year-old daughter, my younger brother, and his German wife—our mini clan—sat around the dining room table. In the raspberry red room, like a sensual womb that swallowed up the family, everyone's faces reflected a rosy glow of health.

"What have you decided to do with Alex and his vaccinations?" my father asked me, as we stuffed our faces with turkey, mashed potatoes, gravy, cranberry sauce.

"We're leaning against vaccinating him," I said. "There are lots of toxins in those shots: mercury, aluminum, lead. I don't want to inject them in his body."

"What crazy idea have you gotten in your head?" he said. "He could be crippled from polio."

"Polio has almost been eradicated in this country," I replied.

"It's people like you who make the world a dangerous place. I remember classmates getting polio, and they could never walk again," he said.

"Alex isn't going to daycare so he has little chance of spreading a disease, or for that matter catching one," I said. "And it makes no sense—if vaccinated children are so well protected, how can an unvaccinated child harm them?"

"You're a public menace," he said. "People like you will bring back small pox!"

I was appalled at my father's vehemence and outburst at a family holiday. This was so unusual for him. He was a Zen Buddhist.

"Where's Baby Love?" my grandmother asked, interrupting the showdown between my father and me.

I got up to look for the furry grey cat.

My grandmother stood up and took out her James Bond-like cane from her purse that hung around her neck at all times. The cane snapped into shape automatically.

"Baby Love," she wailed. "Baby Love, come to mama."

She tapped her way down the narrow hallways of the large house and looked in the many dark crannies where a cat could be hiding.

George got up to help. I picked up Alex. We searched the new part of the house with its large glass windows and light streaming through the rooms. We circled back through the old and new parts of the house. Alex was wide eyed, his synapses multiplying as he absorbed his environment during this concentrated cat search. Click, click, click, we heard my grandmother searching. It was getting dark outside. We couldn't find the cat in my father's castle.

Everyone's nerves were shot.

"Grandmom, I found your cat," George said. She skipped to her bedroom with pink and white candy striped wallpaper. We all followed, eager for the search to be over.

"Baby Love," she whispered and grabbed the cat sleeping on her bed. She was startled. So were we. George had taken one of my little sister's stuffed cats that looked identical to her Himalayan and placed it on my grandmother's bed. He had played a terrible trick. Grandmother dropped her cane and collapsed in a chair, defeated and exhausted.

Then Baby Love sauntered in like an actor on cue, rubbed himself against my grandmother's leg, purring, and jumping on her lap. Reunited, they would not part from one another again during the whole visit. Still, Baby Love had full reign of my father's house.

I was disturbed by my father's strong view on vaccinations. I was pretty sure he hadn't done any research, but he carried so much authority in his point of view. My inner compass knew George and I would not vaccinate Alex. We felt it was the right thing to do. George had been adamant with the doctors against circumcision. We both agreed: Less was more. Nature didn't need to be improved on, whether it was the immune system or a penis.

CHAPTER 6
FASCINATION

"I went through hell and saw there love's raging fire, and I entered heaven illumined with the light of love."

~ Hazrat Inayat Khan

Leaving behind the smells of curry, mango lassis, and fried samosas emitting from the first floor of an Indian restaurant near Union Square, I entered the upstairs private banquet room where Harold Thompson taught his homeopathy classes. The owner of the restaurant, a man from Delhi, was Harold's patient, and gave him the space for a discount. Homeopathy was an acceptable medical practice in India, which I learned many years later.

The class had six people, two men and four women, mostly in their 30s and 40s. I arrived last and sat at the large, table-clothed, dining table, next to Marie, tall and thin dressed in New York black. This was supposed to be a beginner's class, but the questions seemed much more advanced than my knowledge.

"Is Lachesis a right-sided remedy?" Carol, a blond dressed in a chartreuse matching sweater outfit, asked.

She seemed to be from the Upper West Side.

"Did Hahnemann really believe that he was exempt from the psoric miasm?" challenged Peter, who was sporting overalls that gave him the look of a plumber.

OK, Dr. Samuel Hahnemann discovered homeopathy and he came from Germany, but psoric miasm ... Please, what were they talking about?

Marie said with a slight British accent or maybe South African, "This is the book you must own, *Homoeopathic Materia Medica*, by William Boericke, M.D." as she showed her well-worn copy. If this had been a cocktail party full of strangers, I would have approached her first. She pointed to the page with "Lachesis mutus, Bushmaster or Surucucu" written at the top. I read:

> Like all snake poisons, Lachesis decomposes the blood, rendering it more fluid; hence a hæmorrhagic tendency is marked. Purpura, septic states, diphtheria, and other low forms of disease, when the system is thoroughly poisoned and the prostration is profound. The modalities are most important in guiding to the remedy. Delirium tremens with much trembling and confusion. Very important during the climacteric and for patients of a melancholic disposition. Ill effects of suppressed discharges. Diphtheritic paralysis (Botulinum). Diphtheria carriers. Sensation of tension in various parts. Cannot bear anything tight anywhere.

"I like to read this book in the bathroom," she said.

Who *were* these people?

To me, that passage on Lachesis sounded like it came from another century, when they used treatments such as leeches, mercury, and bloodletting.

Harold, in his fifties, scruffy looking, taught in a free-form style, where students jumped in with what I thought were random questions.

Harry, in his late thirties from Staten Island, talked like he was a member of the Italian mob. "I gave my wife that Sepia in 200c ... She's been less bitchy. She even wanted to have sex this week," he said.

I remembered that remedy from Harold's lecture at the Open Center. Does that mean the remedy worked? I could imagine an independent woman with lots of children, stuck at home, no longer desiring her husband.

Harold finally called the class to order. He was going to teach us how to take a case. "Take out your Kent's *Repertory of the Homoeopathic Materia Medica*," he said.

Marie opened a 4-inch thick black book, printed on thin rice-like paper with thumb print indentations labeled: Mind, Genitalia, Extremities, Sleep, Generalities, in no particular order that I understood. She scooted closer to me so we could share the book with its six-point font.

"Who can find: desires salty food?" asked Harold.

Marie found it in an instant. Clearly, I was sitting next to the Ph.D. student.

"What are the remedies listed?" he asked.

She read natrum muriaticum, argentum nitricum, cocculus indicus. I saw cryptic abbreviations like nat mur, arg nit, cocc.

"What can you tell me about these remedies?"

"Some are in bold, others are in italic, and others are in plain text," Carol competed for his attention. "Bold gets a number 3, italic 2, and plain 1."

"Correct, and I want you to pass out these repertorization sheets," he said. "You'll need the forms for figuring out the remedy to prescribe."

Carol jumped out of her seat to pass the spreadsheet-like papers around. Harold gave her a smile showing off all of his teeth—his way of flirting with his female students.

"In the left column, write out all the rubrics of your client, be sure to cover mind symptoms, generals, as well as physical symptoms," he said.

"What is a rubric?" I asked, never shy to look stupid in front of others.

"Hey Teach, me too, what's a rubric? Is that the same thing as a symptom?" asked Harry.

"It is the exact translation of the patient's expressions into repertorizable symptoms," Harold answered. "Symptoms that can be found in the Materia Medica."

"Oh, boy. So, I write down the problems in the left column," said Peter.

"Then you look up the rubrics in the repertory and write out the remedies listed and put their names in the narrow columns at the top of the page," Marie said.

Who was teaching this class?

"Yes, and then as Carol said, if the remedy is a 1, 2, or 3, write it in the square next to the rubric," said Harold. "Ignore any rubric that has more than 30 remedies listed."

"Why?" I asked.

"In homeopathy, we are looking for the strange, rare, and peculiar—not common symptoms like headaches, but like stabbing occipital pain, on left side, better from pressure and worse at 3 p.m.," he explained.

Class was over. I wrote down the names of the books, took several copies of the case-taking sheets, and hung around, not quite ready to leave. I loved challenges. This was quirky, too.

"Where can I buy these books?" I asked Marie.

"You can borrow mine, I have several copies at home," Marie offered. The other copies must have been waiting for her in the bathroom, where she would study away from her children.

"Thank you," I said. I had made a friend.

* * *

I walked home, excited to try this new exercise on George. He would be my first patient. It sounded like fun, like astrology. Maybe I would gain some insights. Still, practicing medicine after my first class was outlandish. No, this was a parlor game. The joke was on me, thinking this homeopathy thing was more than an experiment in off the wall ideas.

George kissed me at the front door. He was happy to see me. Alex was asleep in our bedroom. Could I really treat Alex if he got sick? Dr. Buten had thought that was normal. Would homeopathy change my ideas of medicine?

"George, what's bothering you? I'm going to take your case.

Find you a homeopathic remedy. Your constitutional," I said. I learned that a constitutional remedy was like your signature remedy, individual for you, and would treat whatever illness you have.

"I'm tired. You know me, you answer the questions," he said. George had worked all day and looked after Alex so I could go to my first class on homeopathy.

"OK, sometimes you get stomach aches, you fart, have lots of gas," I said.

I looked up gas in abdomen and there were over a 100 remedies listed. I looked down, and there were 30 remedies for cases of feeling worse after eating. I wrote the info on the photocopied sheet from class.

"Irritated in the middle of the night," I said.

"What?" he asked.

"You know, you're a bear if Alex wakes you up in the middle of the night."

"OK, maybe."

"Oh, I know you have cravings for nuts," I said, as George unshelled another pistachio nut and dropped the shells into a bowl on the side table next to the couch.

"You're better for movement."

"What does that mean?" he asked.

"Well, when you get upset you like to go for a walk," I said. "And messy, how do I translate that into a rubric?"

"I'm not messy!"

"Look at your desk."

I wrote out all the symptoms I wanted cured. It was my list after all. I threw in some really strange, rare, and peculiar ones like the out-of-body experience he had in his twenties before he met me. Harold made a big deal about finding those rubrics. I was getting the hang of this repertorizing.

I had a list of 20 remedies across the top of the page. I filled in 1s, 2s, and 3s based on the characteristics of the font. It took hours to record the information on the chart—flipping the tissue thin paper, reading the miniscule abbreviations, holding the book down with my thumb, and making notes. Then, I added up all the columns, and the highest number would be the remedy I would prescribe. Easy.

Fifteen was the highest score. The remedy was Phosphorus. I looked in my homeopathic kit. There was the blue bottle. The label on the bottle said it was for dizziness with headaches, something George didn't have. What harm could there be? There was nothing in these medicines. They tasted like candy. George would be my guinea pig.

"Sweetie, take this," I filled the cap with 2 to 3 white pellets the size of BBs.

"Open your mouth," I said. He obliged. He was a risk taker when it came to new medicines.

I poured the pellets under his tongue. This was the second time I had used a homeopathic remedy in my life. I didn't know if the remedy my doula gave me during labor had done anything. Everything had gone so quickly at that time. I never asked the doula what remedy she had prescribed.

"It's sweet," George said.

"Yes, the pellets are milk sugar. Phosphorus is a mineral found in plants. It's diluted and succussed," I said.

"Succussed?" he asked.

"Pounded or shaken—it's like you're getting a drop of phosphorus in an ocean all tumbled around," I told him.

"Oooooh, oooooh," George moaned loudly.

He had doubled over. "My stomach's cramping. It's too painful. What's in this stuff?" he asked.

"It can't be the remedy. There's nothing in them."

I helped him to our queen-sized bed. He curled up into a fetal position, moaning. His forehead was perspiring. I brought him a glass of water. He was in too much pain to sit up and drink. Alex woke up, and I coaxed him back to sleep.

"Ooooooh," he cried.

Within seconds of taking the remedy, my husband was having the worst reaction I had ever seen. I heard that coffee was an antidote for remedies, reversing their effects. I made him a cup of coffee and forced him to sip it. The pain slowly tapered off after an hour. He slept deeply through the night.

This was a new paradigm, this homeopathy world. I saw a remedy act on a real person. I was blown away. This was not possible. If I had not seen it myself, I would have explained it away. I would think it was Marguerite's meatloaf. Yet he had never been sick from her dinners before. He had stomach cramps in the past, but these came out of nowhere and were much more intense than any pain he had before. Clearly, the remedy had done this to him. I remembered Harold talking about aggravations as a good thing. Was this an aggravation? Did the coffee do anything to help?

George fell asleep before I could ask him what he thought.

The next morning, George woke up with lots of energy. He said he had had a fabulous dream of rowing on the Mediterranean Sea like when he was a boy spending summers with his grandparents on Tinos. His eyes looked brighter.

"I feel great," he announced. "You're going to become a homeopath."

My sweet George. He always knew how passionate I could become about a project or making a close friend—long before I was aware of what was happening.

At the next homeopathy class, I explained what had happened.

"What! You gave him coffee?" Harold said. "You weren't supposed to do that."

"But he was in pain."

"It would have passed. It was an aggravation. What splendid results! You found your husband's constitutional remedy," he said.

"Constitutional remedy?" I asked wanting to hear his definition again.

"Yes, the remedy that will support him to get better on all levels: mentally, physically, emotionally, even spirituality," he said.

I didn't understand any of this. I had administered a medicine as implausible as a black hole, and it made the patient sick, then better. I was fascinated. I bought every book on homeopathy I could find. George was eager to hear all about any discovery I made. This medical modality fit the energy medicine paradigm he had studied at the IM School of Healing Arts. I was embarrassed by my early dismissal of his studies, as I became more and more immersed in my homeopathic studies.

* * *

A year later, I was still going to Harold's beginner's classes. There really was only one weekly class that he taught regularly. And there were no other homeopathy courses in New York City at the time. We were the same seven students attending what Harold called The New York School of Homeopathy. There was no homework, tests, or graduations. I no longer slept during Alex's nap. Studying homeopathy became a part-time job.

Alex no longer wanted to ride in his stroller. As soon as he could walk, he wanted to explore the material world; every fire hydrant, crack in the street, and concrete apartment stoop held immense clues to the world he lived in. I was deep in exploring these spirit-like medicines—as eager to understand them as Alex was to learn about the nature of objects.

During Alex's playgroups, when he climbed the dome-like structures with the other kids in the playground, I read Boericke's *Homoeopathic Materia Medica*—looking up remedies I didn't know. I began prescribing homeopathic remedies—Arnica for minor falls, Hyland's Baby Teething Tablets for new dentition, Oscillococcinum for first signs of the flu. In New York, my crowd was open to alternative medicine and trusted me. If I suggested a homeopathic remedy, they were willing to give it a try.

But with my father and brother, who was going to medical school, I had to defend homeopathy. They pointed out the absurdity of its premise.

"There is nothing in those remedies," my brother said.

"Nobody's heard of this homeopathy thing," my father said.

I was trying to ignore the implausibility. I knew these medicines worked.

* * *

"We will be doing a proving," Harold told the class in a bland white chiropractor's waiting room on West 33rd Street, our new class location.

"My homeopathic colleagues and I will run the proving. First, we'll take your cases as a base point, then you will be given the remedy in 30c. You will not know what it is. We are following a double blind procedure so some of you may get a placebo. Your homeopath for the proving will check in with you daily to record your new symptoms."

I was excited. Provings were the way that new remedies became part of our Materia Medica, our homeopathic pharmacy. The new recorded symptoms induced by taking a remedy would become part of the repertory. Now, I had reverence for this medical modality. This new adventure would allow me to enter the world of a remedy from the inside, and discover a remedy from experiencing it firsthand.

"Can my husband join in?" I asked.

"Yes, of course. We're always looking for volunteers," he said.

* * *

George and I were driving to my dad's place each month to participate in a new intentional community forming in Cambridge, Massachusetts, called Cornerstone Village Cohousing. We started to envision our lives out of New York City. We were transitioning from the pulsating bohemian life to the rhythms of a full family life. Our needs were changing—we wanted to live with other families with children and older people, have more space, and still be part of an intentional community with shared facilities. My grandmother was going to help with the down payment, and move in with us.

Since I left home at seventeen years old, I had looked for communities to join. First, it was the film and artist community, the women's community in Manhattan, then the Penington Quaker community, now it was cohousing. I wanted to feel that I was part of an extended family that understood me. Cohousing communities were beginning to be built across the United States. The idea came from Denmark, where the homes were designed for "people who want to own an apartment but not feel shut off by it, lost in an impersonal city," quoted in *The New York Times*.

On this trip to the Boston area, we would be going to a Cornerstone meeting, staying with family, and visiting friends while participating in this proving. It was Memorial Day weekend. We had left my grandmother at the Penington with her aide because she didn't want to go on a long road trip.

"What do you think will happen?" George asked, while driving exactly 55 MPH on Highway 95 North to Concord, Massachusetts. I was relaxed, as we listened to the soft rock radio station. George was the safest driver I knew.

"We can take the remedy tonight. I have it with me," I said. "Then tomorrow we'll call the homeopaths who are supervising the proving to check in."

"That woman who took my case was strange. She asked a zillion random questions, like did I sleep on my right side or left side?" he said. "Why did I have to go through that?"

"Harold wants a baseline so they record all the rubrics that are particular to you. The proving is looking for the strange, rare, and peculiar symptoms that are new symptoms that you've never had before," I told him. Alex was asleep in his car seat. He would nod off on car trips.

We arrived safely at my dad's home at night. We tucked Alex in the bed between us. We still did a family bed so I could easily nurse him at night. I gave George the unmarked sugar pills in the bottle cap. He took four pellets. I did the same.

"You're sure you don't know what this is?" he asked.

"No idea."

We fell asleep immediately after I nursed Alex.

In the morning, Alex, twenty months old, woke up and sat up straight. George and I were still asleep on either side of him.

"Daddy, my milkie," he said, looking straight at my breasts, as I woke up.

"OK, dear," I said.

When he was done, he said "Mommy." Then turned around and climbed into George's arms and hugged his father's bare chest.

George spoke to Alex in Greek. Their special language. Alex understood everything but would answer in English.

There was no hesitation in Alex's voice. Our son had swapped our genders. I was daddy, and George was mommy!

"This must be the remedy," I said.

"Whoa, this is so weird," George said.

"We'll have to tell the homeopaths. Wonder what's next?" I mused.

Provings were known to alter reality, create feelings and circumstances not experienced before, produce new symptoms, usually short lived. Dreams were also important. It was like going to a foreign country—everything looked different. You were still you, just acting differently, and different things would happen. I was excited about how quickly the remedy had taken affect. Alex got a dose through my breast milk. Were we homeopathic explorers, discovering new healing substances?

* * *

Later, George drove us further north on Highway 95 to visit friends who had a summer place in New Hampshire. The Beatles were playing on the radio. Across three lanes, we saw a black VW bug heading for the next right exit. Suddenly, the VW swerved across all the lanes and passed a few feet in front of us to get off on the right exit.

I gasped. George kept the car going straight in the slow lane.

"Man, that was close," said George.

A few minutes later, a car zigzagged in front of us. George leaned on the car horn, warning the driver. I was shaking. George started to speed up and passed him. He gave the driver the finger. George had never done anything like that before.

"Why'd you do that?" I asked.

"Don't tell me anything, that driver deserved it," he said.

On our way back from seeing our friends, we drove behind a white van that jostled over something on the nearly empty highway. Fifty feet ahead of us, the van's bumper was lying on the road.

George maneuvered around the fallen car part.

"Fuck!" George shouted.

Over the next month, George tailgated cars. He cursed at drivers that drove too close to him.

"*Malaka*," he told an old lady driver, which is "wanker" in Greek.

"That could have been grandmom," I said. He didn't care. It was as if that remedy took possession of him every time he got in the car.

Some of the drivers followed us and honked at us, after George gave them the finger.

"George, you must stop this. Someone is going to pull out a gun and shoot us," I said.

"No, it's not me. It's YOU. You're so jumpy in the car," he said.

The peaceful man I knew had become a menace in the car.

I told my homeopath supervisor what was happening. George's homeopath had quit because she got busy so George was no longer part of the proving.

"This must be the remedy. What remedy zips around caring less about where they're going?" I asked. "And has a terrible attitude!"

"It's not the remedy. I have a prover who has road rage, and the remedy didn't cure him," she said. The homeopath was talking about the homeopathic principle of "like cures like." In theory, in order to heal a disorder, a remedy would be given for the same condition that was produced in a proving. The first remedy discovered by Dr. Hahnemann was China officinalis. After he took the Peruvian bark, known to cure malaria, in an accidental proving, he experienced intermittent fevers and other malaria-like symptoms. Hahnemann hypothesized and confirmed that China officinalis was effective in treating malaria because it also produced the symptoms similar to those of malaria.

"You think?" I said, not sure I could accept her explanation. In Hahnemann's *Organon of Medicine*, the homeopath's bible, there was also the idea of totality of symptoms. You didn't give a remedy for one condition but for a cluster of symptoms that matched the remedy picture. This homeopathy had so many rules and illogical ideas. I was suspecting homeopaths didn't know everything about homeopathy.

Another week into this proving, I felt a heavy cloak of depression wrap around me. I was walking down 3rd Avenue with Alex holding my left hand and my grandmother linking arms on my right side. This thick, impenetrable energy came up from behind like the presence of a stranger too close to my back and sucked all the vitality out of my body. I barely made it home and then collapsed on the couch for two days. Alex was good natured. He watched *Teletubbies* on TV when I couldn't function. I was zombie-like, unable to think, barely able to walk, and profoundly disinterested in everything. This time, my supervisor said this collapsed state was the proving.

"The remedy grabbed you for sure," she said.

At the end of the month we all gathered in the Penington parlor for the final proving meeting to share the results. George stayed home with Alex, since he was no longer a prover.

"So what is this remedy?" I asked. My curiosity was bursting. I gave my summary of what had been happening to our family to the proving group.

"It was like my life had been kidnapped for the past month. Our son is back to normal calling me 'Mommy' and George 'Daddy.' I now have a glimpse of what it's like for people who live with depression. So much more compassion for them. It was like I had been an actor living someone else's life. I am so glad it's over."

"The remedy is Musca domestica, the common house fly," Harold told us, like he was announcing the winner on *The Price Is Right*.

"We took the fly remedy?" I asked.

"Yuk, that's disgusting," said Marie.

"The fly has an androgynous existence," he said.

"Perhaps Alex's mixing up our gender is related to this androgyny," I said.

Harold continued. "Its vision is kaleidoscopic so the fly moves in irregular ways."

Marie turned to me. "Maybe George's crazy driving and those

zigzagging cars you keep seeing are also an aspect of this fly remedy," she said. "It's all that Doctrine of Signature."

"Shhh," I whispered when the provers turned to stare at Marie and me.

I couldn't fathom this Doctrine of Signature. How could these random events be related to taking a highly diluted and succussed fly?

"What about road rage?" I asked the group. I wasn't going to let it go. Especially since George was still driving in an aggressive manner after taking the remedy.

"Not related to this remedy, but your other symptoms will be included in the Materia Medica," my supervisor homeopath assured everyone.

After the proving, George and I were constantly fighting in the car when he drove. He ran red lights, cursed out loud. I was fed up. I was hyper alert, startled every time he pressed the gas too hard or stopped suddenly.

Then, he ran a stop sign and blurted out, "It's that damn remedy!"

This spontaneous realization and affirmation was finally voiced out loud. His driving returned to normal. Proving symptoms usually stopped when there was an intention by the group that the proving was over. George had been stuck in proving limbo. His declaration must have been his way of ending his proving symptoms. But I never fully recovered. More than fifteen years later, I still get anxious in the car when he drives.

My dilemma after this proving, this Doctrine of Signature, pushed deep into my sub-conscious. The implications of substances holding a complex archetype that could be studied was too much for me. A housefly possessing the medicine power of the animal was also beyond my comprehension, but the idea that the proving would bring out a range of symptoms, homeopathic Materia Medicas, and modern repertories would be updated with this new information made sense.

Homeopathy was becoming my calling. I couldn't explain how filmmaking, which had been my life until now, was being replaced by this holistic health modality. This was more than a career change.

At Harold's first lecture, what had caught my attention was

when he spoke about homeopathy and spirituality. This merging of concepts created new synapses in my brain. There were connections I could not deny. Psychology, medicine, unseen realities, and energy substances were kaleidoscopes making new patterns. How could I make sense of this new paradigm?

CHAPTER 7

SYNCHRONICITY

"I wept in love and made all weep with me."

~ Hazrat Inayat Khan

The chanting of the Koran filled the ancient market in Morocco. My father, my twelve-year-old half-sister Olivia, nearly three-years-old Alex, and I wandered through the dark tunnels of Marrakesh where wooden thuja boxes with secret locks, leather bridles, sacks of spices, and iron chains were sold. Olivia was on a winter break, and my father was splurging on a trip to Morocco.

Our guide took us deeper and deeper into the dark caverns of commerce, where the canopied path was shaded and cool. Then, we saw light at the end of the tunnel. The guide bid us goodbye. We walked out into the open square, in search of a taxi to take us back to the hotel for lunch, all of our sensations overloaded like we had been visiting a museum for hours. Our eyes blinked, adjusting to the North African sun. I turned to see Alex frozen still—a black snake wrapped around his neck.

"*Arrête ! Qu'est-ce que tu fais?*" I motioned to the snake charmer to remove the snake. Instead, the grimacing, wiry Moroccan added two more snakes, thicker and bigger than the first one, on my son's shoulders.

Alex stared at me mutely. His eyes implored me to stop this from happening to him.

"*Maintenant!* Take them off!" The man either understood my French or my distress. He grabbed his snakes and deposited them into a basket. The serpents slithered.

I wasn't afraid of snakes. Ouroboros, the mythic archetypal symbol of the serpent eating its tail, invokes synthesis in action. For Carl Jung and the alchemists, snakes were a symbol of assimilation, the merging of duality and immortality. Jung gave importance to unusual happenings that carried meaning. This snake encounter in Marrakesh evoked the memory of when I dropped into the abyss.

* * *

On the return flight from Morocco, my father, sister, and Alex slept. We had a fun time in the sun touring Marrakesh, Essaouira, and Casablanca, but the image of the snakes around Alex's neck haunted me. A dark and evil creature had touched me in the past.

When I was 24 years old, I lived through my dark night of the soul. It culminated when I was sitting in hot water in a bathtub. I felt a completely foreign being inside me uncurl, open its mouth, and let out a cry, a primordial scream, as if the thing knew the pain of being human, of being a failure, of living with the unknown. This being was otherworldly, an alien, shouting a message I couldn't understand. It was a growl, a release. Minutes felt like hours. Then, this invader left me as suddenly as it had grabbed me. I was free of its bond. This unconscious reptile held me captive no longer. My fragile mask fell and shattered. I was raw, no pretenses. I had realized that my labels—war correspondent, filmmaker, girlfriend, fiancée, lesbian, bisexual, fatso—were meaningless. They were not me. Before this crisis, I had felt hopeless, worthless, and lonely. The moan I exhaled in the bathtub, soaking in hot water, had no power over me. I could no longer hate myself for being fat, for making a mistake, for my failures, for who I was.

The night we returned to New York from the weeklong vacation in Morocco, Alex woke up with a fever. In the middle of holding vigil for Alex, I told George about the snakes and my memory of my dark night of the soul. I was grateful for the release that came from the creature I expelled, which opened me to experience life where I made better choices—not pursuing a standard lifestyle. I married a Greek man who followed my lead of an independent life—a creative life, a spiritual life, a family life. I explored his journey into alternative healings, the occult, the super natural.

We had more years together than I had lived without him. Our histories merged. We carried the milestones of ourselves and each other in our hearts and souls. Alex's childhood was part of our expansion and complex histories.

The hero's journey was too simplistic. The individual overcoming challenges to return home did not tell the whole story. George and I were a team, we had layers of memories cycling around, themes of dark and light revealed and integrated. Our stories played out like the fairy tale three doors. Which door would we open and enter to reveal a new passage and more secrets?

In the morning, Alex was still coughing. George took his temperature, 102 degrees. He was concerned.

"Call the doctor," he said.

I called our homeopath, Rose. I had taken Alex to her when he was a baby. At eight months, Alex had astounded both of us when he spoke his first word, "Buddha," in her office, pointing to a bronze Buddha statue on her top shelf. Rose was British and trained in England. She was going to open a homeopathy school in New York in the fall, and I planned to attend.

Rose prescribed Tuberculinum 30c. (made from a tubercular abscess) on the phone for Alex's fever. I took the remedy out of the Boiron homeopathic kit I had bought after Alex's birth.

"Put 2 to 3 pellets in a glass of water, stir 10 times, and give him a teaspoon as often as needed," she said.

His fever came down, but his cough was getting worse. It started to have a strange whooping sound. I called her back, and she changed the remedy. Drosera 30c (made from sundew, a carnivorous plant) administered in the same way. I had to repeat the remedy often, but each time his cough stopped for a few hours at a time.

I took Alex to the nurse practitioner. She diagnosed him. He had pertussis, whooping cough, so she prescribed an antibiotic and cough suppressant. Full confirmation would take two weeks, but she recommended immediate quarantine and treatment. My father's rant that an unvaccinated child could be a menace to society had happened. For the next two months, Alex would not be allowed to play at his Waldorf toddler program. I never filled the prescriptions and only used homeopathy. Alex recovered quickly.

Since I saw how Drosera acted immediately each time he started to cough, I knew the remedy was working. Alex was not suffering. He slept longer than usual. All indications were that he was getting better and better each day. I understood from my homeopathic studies that symptoms were the best way for the body to come back into balance. By suppressing symptoms with cough suppressants and antibiotics, the illness could drag out longer. I trusted Rose and homeopathy because I could see the difference. If Alex had been getting sicker, I would have given him the antibiotics—but there was no need.

I had assumed that Alex caught the cough in Morocco. But later I discovered that many children in his Waldorf playgroup had whooping cough-like symptoms, even though they had been vaccinated. The incubation period of whooping cough was 7 to 10 days. Could he have caught this disease from the immunized children?

* * *

Alex was growing up. I had weaned him the previous fall. He had raged at my insistence that he drink milk from a bottle instead of my breast. George had wanted him weaned, and most of the parenting books were in agreement that two years of breastfeeding was long enough. But after Alex's protest, we both decided that the next time he wanted to nurse, I would give my breast to him. Alex never asked to be nursed again.

When Alex had nearly recovered from whooping cough, George's friends, Kostas and his wife, Heleni, called us out of the blue, inviting us for dinner. They didn't like me so we never saw them. They held a grudge from the time George and I broke up during our ten-year long-distance relationship before we married. George told them Alex was being quarantined because of whooping cough. They insisted we bring him. George relented. He thought we could reconnect and become friends again.

Kostas and Heleni spoke in Greek so I could not participate in the conversations. I felt excluded. Alex coughed with that distinctive whooping cough, while Heleni ran to the kitchen. I saw her eyes tear up. I repeated Alex's homeopathic remedy, and he fell asleep. I wanted to go home after this strange incident and their rudeness at dinner.

I went to the car, strapped Alex in his car seat, then turned up the heat and waited for George. He was taking a long time to say goodbye.

When he finally got into the driver's seat, he said, "Kostas told me they lost a son to whooping cough."

"How could that be?" I said. "Did they say anything at dinner? I couldn't understand any of it."

"No, not at all. Only when you left," George said. "They told me their son was Alex's age. His name was Iannis. They left him in his crib in his bedroom. The doctors advised this so that they could sleep better. He died in the middle of the night. They found him the next morning—his body was blue, cold."

"I can't imagine how awful that must have been for them. And all the memories we stirred up," I said.

"They said they wanted us there to help them grieve, to face what happened. They could never talk about their son until after they called us," he said.

"This is so sad," I said.

Twice, George and I had followed parenting advice from experts. Let your child cry himself to sleep. Don't give in if you are to wean your baby. Be strong. Both times we felt what we were doing was wrong. We went against our instincts, felt like we caused unnecessary trauma. Two basic functions, feeding and sleeping, were being tampered with by following outside advice. We didn't allow our son to guide us. I wished I had listened to Alex's needs and not followed the cultural norm.

The doctor's advice for Kostas and Heleni seemed as reasonable as the advice we followed, but in their case it had dire consequences. Maybe if they were sleeping next to their son, they would have realized what was happening and been able to get help. Antigone, George's mother, had been given advice by her doctor to make no contact with her second son at birth because he was born premature and was not expected to live. Marios did survive. Spiro, his father, could not stay away and went to the hospital. When he held his son for the first time, Marios began to thrive. What would have happened to George's only brother if Spiro had not followed his heart?

* * *

At the Penington, Marguerite served green gazpacho made with green grapes, sweet and tangy, and a tomato mozzarella salad in the dining room. I was going to miss our little peace of Manhattan. We were moving to Bensonhurst in Brooklyn, into a four-bedroom apartment. Cornerstone Village Cohousing, the intentional community in Cambridge, Massachusetts, was taking much longer to come together than we had planned. Cohousing was a new concept in the neighborhood, and the project had run into serious zoning problems.

Alex, three-years-old, was running now. We needed more space. I still loved being his mom. Alex's world of toys and new adventures were met with joy and openness. He ran back to include George and me in each discovery.

"See this, Mom," he said. "Dad, over here—come here." He giggled with delight at the awesomeness of life. The depth of my love was immense and expanded in the ordinariness of basic chores caring for him.

Alex ran to his great-grandmother who leaned over to hug him. My grandmother, dressed in her favorite white linen dress, wore her signature amber necklace with fossils and dead insects embedded in the golden resin. Her white leather Chanel purse was strapped around her neck. She sat next to Paul, who looked like Tweedle Dee in his striped red shirt and suspenders, with his pants pulled up high over his belly.

"I'm not moving," my grandmother said. She was glaring at me with a don't-you-dare-argue-with-me-young-lady-I'm-the-elder-here look.

"Why?" George asked.

"I'm just NOT going," she said.

"Eunice, maybe we could—" Paul said.

"They will not understand. These young folks—they only think of themselves," she said.

Alex was laughing. My friend Emily, who noticed everything that needed fixing at the Penington but was eager to distract Alex from the argument, was tickling him at the other end of the table.

We had recently returned from our annual summer trip to Greece and noticed something different between my grandmother and Paul. They were more of a couple than before. Samantha, the manager, told me she had seen Eunice leave Paul's bedroom in the morning before breakfast while we were gone. My grandmother told me they had had a great time visiting museums, movies, and going to concerts in the park. She was happy.

"Grandmom, you can stay here if you want," I said.

"That's right. I'm living here at the Penington—with Baby Love!" she said.

* * *

George, Alex, and I settled into our new apartment in Bensonhurst, Brooklyn. I was driving through the Battery Tunnel to Manhattan every few days to visit my grandmother. Alex counted as a person, sitting high up in his booster seat, so we glided past all the congested traffic in the HOV lane.

This morning Samantha called me—she was worried about my grandmother.

"Eunice didn't come down for dinner last night or breakfast this morning," she said.

I found my grandmother in bed without her lipstick but her purse safely posed on her chest. Paul was sitting in the chair by her bedside. She had a fever and was coughing. My grandmother had a susceptibility for pneumonia.

In her first month of arrival at the Penington, she had spent three weeks in the hospital and the next two months in her bedroom recovering from pneumonia. The next year, she had pneumonia again. I had called Rose, who prescribed Arsenicum 30c (made from arsenic). My grandmother was released from the hospital after a week and fully recovered in less than a week after that.

I called Rose this day. She prescribed Arsenicum 200c in water, to be repeated as needed. Potencies were an enigma in homeopathy. The 200c indicated a stronger potency than the previous 30c, more dilution and succussion increased the power of the remedy. The elderly, who had less vital power, usually needed lower potencies, but not my robust grandmother.

She was a textbook case of Arsenicum: anxious, restless, fastidious, an aristocratic type, likes to collect things, high standards (especially in a material sense), a perfectionist at work, likes to look chic, paranoid about being robbed (the reason she wears her purse at all times even during sleep), fear of poverty, thirstless, and prone to being very frightful of death. Arsenicum was also a remedy known to cure pneumonia.

The remedy worked immediately. My grandmother fell asleep and woke up a few hours later without a fever. She wouldn't have to go to the hospital after all, or take antibiotics. I was relieved. This homeopathy rocks!

*　*　*

A week later my throat scratched, then burned and swelled. I ignored the symptoms. I was doing a lot of caretaking driving back and forth to Manhattan for my grandmother, looking after Alex, running around in February, one of the coldest months in the city. I missed living close to the Penington. I felt isolated out in Brooklyn. George and I were worried that we were going to lose our large deposit for our duplex apartment at Cornerstone Village Cohousing, and my grandmother was no longer on board with moving with us to Cambridge away from Paul.

Driving home, I felt feverish. I climbed into bed. My throat started to close. I couldn't sip water without excruciating pain. My fever was 102.

George came home from work and insisted I go to the emergency room. "Why didn't you call your homeopath?" he asked.

"I don't know," I answered, too tired to think.

George asked Deborah, a homeopathic friend who lived nearby, to drive me to the Brooklyn Hospital, while he stayed with Alex. Deborah stretched her long legs and pointed her toes in dancer-like poses, while we sat in the waiting room with fluorescent lights—not speaking. It looked like a war scene. People, much sicker than me, moaned, stared blankly, and sat on garish orange plastic seats waiting their turn at triage, which never seemed to come. One person was lying on a gurney against the wall. The disinfectant and vomit smell was nauseating. A man with a bullet wound was rushed in for treatment, jumping the queue.

After three hours, the nurse in triage took a swab from my throat and confirmed that I had strep throat. The doctor handed me an antibiotic prescription, which we filled at the hospital pharmacy. This diagnosis and treatment took about ten minutes and was paid for by our HMO.

"Why don't you call your homeopath?" Deborah asked me, when the ordeal was over and we were back at my home.

"It's late," I said. "I'll take the antibiotics."

"You take care of everyone else ... and, what, you don't deserve homeopathy?" she chastised me.

I called Rose at 11 p.m. She didn't seem to mind and prescribed the deadly nightshade Belladonna 1M (1000c), four pellets in water repeated as needed. My Boiron homeopathic kit didn't have this potency. Deborah drove to her house and fetched the remedy. She had purchased higher potencies from Bigelow Apothecaries, a pharmacy in downtown Manhattan that carried remedies in all potencies, but was afraid to use them. Clearly, I had a strong vital force. I had never taken a homeopathic remedy that strong, 1:1000 dilution. Even Deborah was impressed. She handed me the teaspoon of water with the dissolved sugar pellets.

As I lay down in my bed, I saw the room go into fractals. My eyes were open, and I saw crystals form in front of my vision. I was hallucinating a cave of bright crystals. The pain evaporated. My fever broke. In the morning, I felt like a new person. I stopped the antibiotics (against medical advice—I was supposed to take them for ten more days). Was the vision a combination of the allopathic and homeopathic remedy? Allopathy is the treatment of disease by conventional means, based on drugs having the opposite effects to the symptoms. Homeopathy uses remedies that have a similar effect of the symptoms, to stimulate the body to cure itself.

* * *

These homeopathic remedies were taking me on a journey far from anything I had known before. As Harold had said, homeopathy was part of a paradigm shift. I started to understand what he had been talking about. Spirituality was a part of my life, contained in daily practices. Medicine had been something I used when needed. Now, there was no separation.

Crystals and fractals, were they the real reality, the building blocks of the cosmos? These crystal patterns, geometrical archetypes, were they showing a metaphysical relationship of the parts to the whole, a principle of oneness underlying geometry? The architecture of all form representing interconnectedness, inseparability, and union—the lover—a conscious reminder of our relationship to the whole. These crystalline structures were like a blueprint for the sacred foundation of all things created. I saw a lattice pattern of crystals, a kind of mathematical perfection and repetition. The Greeks believed the five platonic solids, primal models of crystal patterns that occurred in countless variations throughout the world, symbolized the five elements. Fire was represented by the tetrahedron. Cube was the symbol for earth. Octahedron was for air. Dodecahedron was for spirit. And icosahedron was for water.

A veil had been pulled back, the skin of all matter was removed for a moment so I could see the construct, the armature of all things. The beauty astounded me!

What were these remedies capable of? And what was medicine when it bled into cosmic experiences? Synchronicity, meaningful coincidence, was too simple an understanding.

* * *

In the middle of the night, I startled in my sleep and woke up. We had settled into the white house, as three-year-old Alex liked to call our apartment in Bensonhurst, on the second floor of a wood frame house in Brooklyn. Snow covered the streets. The street lights had a yellow glow around them in the white night. The snowflakes softly blanketed the Italian-American neighborhood on January 30th, 2001.

"Follow me," I heard this disembodied voice.

I got out of bed, left George sleeping, and felt a presence guiding me to my altar at the front of the apartment. This spirit felt benevolent.

"Missy, I've been gone for a long time. It hasn't been easy to be away from you all. I want to make it up to you. I've been in a clinic where there are teachers and healers working on me. I'm now capable of communicating with you," my mother's voice spoke to me. "Please, can you forgive me?"

In the glow of the street lamps, I saw a vision of my mother dressed in white silk, her gown flowing. Her skin was porcelain white, ageless. She stood in a white room where translucent curtains blew gently.

"Your perceptions are real," I heard my mother say. "There are other dimensions. You've been accessing them, and now I can talk to you. You're special and have gone down a path that will heal you and future generations. Look after your sister and brother. They may need your guidance. I love you."

I cried. I gasped. My mother spoke to me from the dead. She had died at 57 years old, too young. She had drunk herself to an early grave. But I knew she was all right now. Our family was OK. I had forgiven her years ago.

A breeze whisked through my altar room. I shivered, then lit a candle and sat in meditation. I took a deep breath. I felt at peace, serene. I lit a stick of Japanese incense. The smoke split into two cords, curling around the stick, like the caduceus—two snakes intertwined around a winged staff carried by Hermes, an Olympian god who was the messenger between the gods and humans and the guide to the underworld.

The sun rose and the golden sunlight streamed through the window. The ephemeral light had a strange brightness, as it reflected off the snow and the white clouded sky, and turned to bright daylight. I walked back to our bedroom. I woke up George.

"Where were you?" he asked.

"It's my mother's birthday, January 30th," I told him. "I had a visitation. My mother came to me with a message that there was life after death—even a detox clinic in the after world!"

"Your mother died over ten years ago," he said.

During the mourning, I walked through the grief—supported by the Gurdjieff practices that taught me to observe my emotions, sensations in the body, to not react or do anything while paying attention. Right after my mother died, I spent three months pacing up and down the Manhattan avenues, healing from the loss of my mother. The volume of the agony eventually turned down to a soft hum and life returned to its vibrant pace.

"George, my mother always loved you," I said. "She knew you were a good guy, a keeper."

"It's too bad your mother never met Alex," he said.

"Or the woman I became—a mother, a healer," I said.

"Maybe she knows you now," he said.

"You could be right."

* * *

My delusion—ghost, and spirit visitations—was a rubric in the homeopathic repertory. It was one of those strange, rare, and peculiar symptoms Rose would use to find my constitutional remedy.

I followed a mystical path. My archetypal mother, embodied in my mother spirit, came to check on me, to ask for forgiveness, to remind me to be there for my siblings. The female energy, unconscious brought into consciousness, touched my heart that morning. Now, I was a mother, with all its responsibilities—doing everything I could not to repeat the pain my mother had caused me and my siblings with her alcoholism, rage, and failed attempts at happiness.

I would risk everything to be a joyful mother, healer, lover. My mother, who had succeeded in the material world—first American female Marshall Scholar at Oxford College in England, first woman economist at the Federal Reserve Board, even Sylvia Plath's roommate and best friend at Smith College—was not a role model for me. I followed my father's sacred path, the footsteps of the seeker, and practiced his Rinzai warrior Zen Buddhism with his teacher Eido Roshi. But I was torn. My father had told me that a woman would have to die first and be reincarnated as a man to experience enlightenment. This seemed so unfair. I could not believe this overt sexism in Buddhism. But how would I find the way?

* * *

A friend of George's from his IM School of Healing had invited us to his apartment to attend Pat Rodegast's channeling of Emmanuel, a benevolent entity that spoke through Pat. After homeopathy expanded my sacred barriers of what's true and possible, I was more open to spirits communicating from other worlds.

Pat's deep male Emmanuel voice, so different from her feisty old lady voice, spoke about how we were all here to live the angel's life on the material plane.

"We're all God living the human existence," he/she said.

Emmanuel's words felt true. Did spirits, like people, come in all types? I listened, trying to decide whether it was wisdom or plain bullshit.

* * *

I had left the Gurdjieff group years ago; I had drifted away from going to group meetings, weekend work sessions, and meeting Sarah, my spiritual teacher. Instead, I now chanted the heart sutra each week at the Zendo on the Upper East Side. I liked the austere room, with bamboo mats on the floor and natural daylight coming through the glass wall of the Japanese garden. The gongs, the chants, the open eyes, the staring at the blank wall were opening me up.

I recited each morning:

> Form is emptiness
> Emptiness is form
> Emptiness is not separate from form
> Form is not separate from Emptiness

Zen practice filled my heart and soul with a new sense of understanding. These teachings pointed to something more than the material world. Was there a connection between my crystal vision, spirit, and form? The Gurdjieff community had not been open to these questions.

The Absolute in Zen, where emptiness and form were not separate, seemed like such an abstract concept. It held the possibility of enlightenment but was intangible, beyond my experience. Strangely, spirit was becoming more tangible. I sought more structure, more security in the Zen tradition to grapple with phenomena. I needed to ground myself in a tradition that didn't overtly explore other psychic spirit realms but acknowledged their existence. I chose a guide, a reverent Zen leader, Eido Roshi, my father's teacher. I thought he would point me in the right direction and could answer my questions. I stepped up my Zen practice after recovering from strep throat.

CHAPTER 8

MIRACLE

"I mourned in love and pierced the hearts of men."
— Hazrat Inayat Khan

Four-year-old Alex and I were seated on a wooden bench in a room filled with over 60 people, most of whom were very ill. We were all dressed in white. The walls were painted a bright blue. A Muzak version of "Ave Maria" played in the room. We were at John of God's Casa de Dom Inacio (the house of St. Ignatius Loyola), a spiritual healing center in Abadiânia, Brazil, waiting in the first chamber to be purified and cleansed. A cleansing and purification ritual before a healing is common in many traditions to raise the vibration level, set an intention, and clear out any negative thoughts, energies, or resistance.

The center attracted all kinds of sick people and devotees. People with stage four cancer, inoperable tumors, autoimmune diseases, came here desperate for a cure. I was there more from curiosity and to see what would happen. George loved the connections and friends he had made in the Casa. We wanted Alex to get a healing for his persistent constipation.

* * *

George was resting at the *pousada*, the guest house a block away, where we were staying. He had been here two years previously after Rose, our family homeopath, prescribed Sulphur 30c. The remedy, of which I first learned about at Harold Thompson's lecture, was meant for inspired souls who had eclectic interests and were more invested in exploring ideas than in reaching results. Their spirit of embracing people of all walks of life, coupled with a general awkwardness, were the key characteristics of this remedy—all aspects of my beloved George. The Sulphur remedy acted right away, initiating him in a new life direction.

After taking the remedy, George sold his entire collection of DVDs on the newly established eBay (getting exorbitant prices for Disney's animation classics). After raising $3,000, he began his quest to find João Teixeira de Faria, rumored to be a gifted healer and powerful medium. One evening, George had called from Abadiânia at my father's house, where Alex and I were staying. On a crackly phone line, I heard George say, "I had surgery."

"What kind of surgery?" I asked, assuming it was some energetic healing from John of God.

"João scraped my eyes with a pen knife. I was fully awake standing there and didn't feel a thing," he said. "For real."

George was nearsighted and had worn glasses since he was ten years old.

"This is not possible. Are you OK?" I asked.

"My eyes are swollen now. There was a doctor there, and she described everything on camera. I have it all on video. John of God removed a brain tumor from the person after me. It's all on my video. Wait till you see it!"

When my father heard me say surgery, he came over to the phone. I told him what George had said.

"He's now the father of the family. What is he thinking? This is crazy!" my father said.

"George, dad's pretty upset. I've got to go now. Are you going to be OK?" I asked.

"Sure, I'll be home in two days. I have these daily herbs I have to take for the next 40 days and no sex," he said.

"No sex? OK. Just come home all in one piece," I said.

When I met George at JFK airport, I could see a bright yellow halo around his head. In the past year, George and I had been working and training with Traci, a medium who read energy fields. I was beginning to see lights around people. When I practiced hands-on healing on my Penington friends, I could see colored, cone-shaped chakras spinning.

This gift felt natural. I was surrounded by friends who trusted me and what I was doing. There were some who were envious. However, George loved my embracing his world of the occult—even celebrated that I had surpassed him in psychic abilities.

At homeopathy school, some classmates were getting annoyed when I described the energy fields around videotaped clients and live clinic patients. I wanted to map some treatments between what I saw in the auras and homeopathic remedies, but I was on my own in this endeavor. My homeopathic colleagues and teachers didn't know what to make of my new clairvoyance and merely tolerated the interruptions in class.

When George returned from the first trip to Brazil, he moved slowly through the customs and passport control exit. He barely wanted to touch me when we hugged. George didn't talk much in the car on our way home to our Bensonhurst apartment. When he entered the living room, he said he couldn't be around computers. My turned-on laptop on the desk, 10 feet away from the sofa, was too much for him to bear in his sensitive state. A fire truck blared its siren. George winced.

"I'm having a hard time assimilating frequencies in the atmosphere," he said.

"George, what frequencies are you talking about?" I asked. "I'm worried. What have you done to yourself?"

"I need sleep," he said and went to bed.

I called Traci to make an appointment for the next day.

"Something's happened to George," I said. "He's not himself."

"Don't worry, the entities are working on him," she said.

Now, I was in a realm I could not explain. I had never seen entities. Pat Rodegast's Emmanuel, well-known in the '70s and '80s among occult enthusiasts like my husband, was the closest I had witnessed to anything like this.

Emmanuel had seemed trustworthy and full of wisdom. His words spoken by Pat were messages that had been repeated by all the great sages, especially the mystic ones like Teresa of Ávila:

> Christ has no body now but yours. No hands, no feet on earth but yours. Yours are the eyes through which he looks compassion on this world. Yours are the feet with which he walks to do good. Yours are the hands through which he blesses all the world. Yours are the hands, yours are the feet, yours are the eyes, you are his body. Christ has no body now on earth but yours.

* * *

In bed with George on the first night of his return at 4 a.m., I was startled awake. I felt a shove, a hard push.

"Hey, are you awake?" I asked.

He didn't stir or wake up.

What had happened? Something wanted me out of our bed. I went to sleep in our guest room.

The next day, we met Traci in her office for an emergency session.

"There's a white, cotton-like bandage around your hara line," she told George, describing her vision.

"What's a hara line?" I asked.

"It's a laser-like line that runs through the center of everyone's bodies. It's like a tuning fork for an individual's life purpose and fulfillment in life," she said.

"What does that mean?" I asked.

"You'll see some big changes," she said. "And Melissa, you're right, those entities that woke you up were sent by John of God. They have more work to do on George."

"I'll sleep in the guest room for the next 37 days," I said.

George acted like he was inside some kind of cocoon that shouldn't be disturbed. He barely spoke during the session and moved slowly like an invalid.

"May you trust God that you are exactly where you are meant to be," Traci quoted Teresa of Ávila.

I felt tested. Could I trust something I did not understand?

* * *

George had asked John of God for a visible operation on his eyes—but he really wanted to experience the mystery of the material world (the knife scraping on his eyeball) collapsing into the invisible world (the hara line that Traci described) in a discernible way. He was fearless when it came to giving his body to science—experimenting with the mystical art, the supernatural, the freak-me-out unrealities that existed.

After 40 days, his nearsightedness improved. However, the more noticeable change was that he no longer seemed like the boyish, zippy-do kind of guy I married. He was more grounded and solid, like he had finally settled into his body. He seemed more mature and content with life. He spoke to Penington neighbors with a newfound wisdom. He explored their psyche, asked deep questions about what was underneath their difficulties. He had become the community therapist.

Our conversations about life were challenging many of my assumptions. George quoted Emmanuel, his disembodied guru, "You are bathed in love every minute of every day, for you ARE love. You cannot love another more than you love yourself and you cannot love GOD more than you love another."

"Is Emmanuel real?" I asked.

"What does it matter? Do you feel his truth?" George asked. "We're in his magnificent love."

George's love, loving wisdom, surrounded Alex and me. "Life is a wondrous opportunity to spread your wings and fly," George said.

"It turns me on when you quote Emmanuel," I said, as George embraced me. We kissed.

"Me, too," Alex said, as we pulled him into our arms and danced as one.

* * *

It was August in Abadiânia, and the middle of Brazil's winter season, but it still felt like summer in this Wild West-like, red-dirt rolling hills land, where dry shrublands blew in the cool breezes. We were here as a family for 40 days. We were traveling with a group of Americans, guided by Catherine, a Brazilian, who had also been George's guide on his first trip. My father's company was doing well, and we had cashed in some stocks he gave us to pay for the trip.

George recovered during the symbolic 40 days, and he wanted to share his experiences with anyone who would listen. I had watched his video of the gruesome surgeries—tumors extracted through nostrils without a single flinch from the standing awake patient, George's eye-scraping drama—over and over with friends. After listening to all of George's stories, I wanted to see for myself what this place was like.

* * *

The first thing that struck me when we arrived in Abadiânia was that my usual poor memory for facts was gone. I could recall over 300 remedies and their symptoms (worse left side, cramping pain at 4 a.m., dreams of snakes, etc.), which I had written out on index cards.

I was studying for my Council for Homeopathic Certification exam, which was taking place on September 15th, 2001. I had already completed more than 750 hours of homeopathic training and had ten cases supervised in preparation for graduating from Rose's homeopathy school, The Homeopathy School of New York. I was on my way to becoming a homeopath.

Homeopathy was re-establishing itself in the United States, after nearly a century of obscurity. Homeopathy had been the medicine of choice by the clergy, intellectuals, and politicians when, in 1855, the American Medical Association stripped away the right to practice it. People as famous as Charles Darwin, eleven American presidents including Lincoln, seven popes, J.D. Rockefeller, Mother

Teresa, and the British royal family had used and advocated for homeopathic treatment. "Homeopathy cures a greater percentage of cases than any other method of treatment. Homeopathy is the latest and refined method of treating patients economically and non-violently," Mahatma Gandhi said. The studying for my homeopathic certification was going to be a breeze here in this magical place.

* * *

Back in the purifying and cleansing chamber with "Ave Maria" playing, the door squeaked open and someone new entered. I heard a strange whoop sound, nothing like Alex's old whooping cough, more like a devilish dog yelp coming from a child. Earlier at breakfast, George and I had overheard a conversation of the owner of the *pousada* saying that a five-year-old boy had a relapse the night before.

"John of God treated that boy yesterday, and he was cured," the owner told the *pousada* guests.

The guests leaned in. George and I turned our chairs to join in the conversation.

"Last night, there was a full moon. Did you hear the dogs?" she asked.

We shook our heads no.

"No? Those village dogs circled my friend's *pousada* where that child and his parents are staying. She called me this morning. Those dogs barked and barked. Then it rained, like one dark cloud rained on her place. Only on her *pousada*. Imagine! Then my friend told me that wretched whooping was back in that little boy."

"Could it be autism, maybe Tourette's?" I asked.

"Possession," she whispered.

"George, do you think that could be true?" I asked, when we got up to leave.

"Anything is possible in John of God's world," he said.

"Maybe," I said.

In the first chamber, Alex and I were instructed to keep our eyes closed. I put my hands over Alex's eyes and repeated the instructions. He sat quietly. I put my hands back in my lap.

With my eyes closed, I saw thousands of white lights. They were like fireflies or little beams darting around the room, as though they were misguided missiles, looking for a place or a being to enter. They felt like malevolent dark forces, and the boy's whooping got louder. I felt as though, if one eye opened, it would be an invitation for those spirits to enter a being. I whispered to Alex, "Keep your eyes closed, dear." I knew he would comply.

Then, a bright wall of light appeared, a large shiny surface. The white darts flew in its direction, absorbed into the greater light. The whooping made one last call, as the final being of light fluttered and entered the wall of light. In the presence of dark and evil forces, I saw the light, a wall of bright light, heal this boy.

"I am quite sure I am more afraid of people who are themselves terrified of the devil than I am of the devil himself." Teresa of Ávila's quote came to my mind.

Later that day, I saw the boy walking cheerfully next to his parents. The *pousada* owner pointed him out. He was chasing a yellow butterfly down the street.

* * *

In Brazil, good and evil forces coexisted and were tangible—catapulting possibilities of transformation, like the healing of the little boy. Carl Jung, in his last writings in *Aion*, described the Quaternio Series of the Self as a person similar to Maslow's self-actualizing person, a human being reaching their full potential. Jung described this process of individualization or self-actualization happening when human beings became transcendent and delve into the unconscious parts of themselves. Maslow believed this achievement was only possible after satisfying basic and mental needs.

Jung wrote, whoever "... culminates above in the idea of a 'light' and good God, so he rests below on a dark and evil principle, traditionally described as the devil or as the serpent that personifies Adam's disobedience." The idea is that our shadow self must become conscious. It would be better for us to know our weaknesses so we are able to recognize our dark side when we act or react from a negative place.

The wall of white light that I saw in the purifying chamber could be Jung's description of a good God. The negative beings that caused the illness in the child could be Jung's idea of Adam's disobedience; (God's punishment for Adam taking a bite of the apple was the discovery of good and evil). When the dark and evil were reunited in the light, there was a healing. These archetypes were too Judeo-Christian for me. My understanding was simpler; there must be a positive force, something indescribable that emanates all around us and through us, that heals and transforms.

The memory of the ecstatic mystery bringing me to the Divine, a positive force, had been embedded in me many years ago, when I was leaving Afghanistan. Grace had descended through me when I had stretched myself beyond my comfort zones. I was shot with a blissfulness that stunned me. I had felt every cell flickering inside me. My body dissolved into the light. There was no me, no car, no driver, no mountain, no sunrise. I was exploding, bouncing, containing all. I was it. This oneness was all there was. There were no boundaries, no time, just this. The sensation was startlingly palpable and a first. I discovered a new truth: that there was an existence infused with a Divine quality that was inspiring, awesome, and life-transforming.

* * *

Alex had struggled with constipation for the last three months in New York. None of the homeopathic remedies Rose prescribed alleviated his several hours of discomfort passing a stool. Sometimes, a week or 10 days went by before he pooped. We brought Alex to John of God for a healing.

John of God worked while in a complete trance. Entities would take over João's body. He had a cast of possibilities as to who would inhabit his body to perform healing miracles. At breakfast, people discussed which entity had treated them. Could it be the spiritual patron of the clinic, Saint Ignatius? Or the new upstart Tibetan lama that was the rave at the moment? Then, there were several surgeons who had existed in previous incarnations. John of God had all of his healing sessions videotaped because he had no memory of what happened during his mediumships. He would review his own work, to see the surgeries he performed when he was taken over by the spirits.

The myth around John of God made it hard to know what was true and what was fiction. He had fallen asleep in a church when he was a young man and woken up to discover that every parishioner had been healed of what ailed them. He was hailed as a mystic healer.

John of God looked into Alex's eyes. He prescribed the same herbs that he suggested to everyone who came to him for treatment. No recommendation for surgery, visible or invisible, or the rainbow-colored lights on a massage table in a private treatment room that George had told me about. Nothing happened that I witnessed.

At night, Alex slept next to us in a single bed in the *pousada* room. In the middle of night, he stirred. I saw him get on all fours like a puppy. I gave him his bottle of milk. He laid down, curled on his side, and went back to sleep.

In the morning, when I changed his night pull-up, I found a brown egg. His excrement was in the shape of a hard egg. I couldn't imagine how he pooped this out without his usual whimpering. He had birthed an egg. Alex never suffered from constipation again.

As a mother, I was grateful that my son would not suffer from this painful condition. Alex was having fun in the village, learning to ride a two-wheeler. He started with training wheels, but soon we saw the little wheels were not rolling on the ground when he biked. Alex was excited by his accomplishment.

"Look at ME, mom. I'm flying!" he shouted, as he rode circles around George and me.

Our days were passing in this village, where we hung out with the *pousada* guests, an eclectic group of travelers: a couple in their twenties, who had come to cure the husband's inoperable malignant brain tumor; a man in his nineties, who was a world traveler looking for longevity; an elderly Scottish father and his son, in his forties, who was in a wheelchair after a massive stroke.

On a walk on the red-dirt, cowboy-like trails, I was searching for crystals that refracted rainbow light from the ground. I bumped into Stuart, the elderly Scottish father who was here for a miracle for his paralyzed son.

"Melissa, whatcha looking for in these trails?" he asked.

"My husband George is hooked on crystals. I was hoping to find him one," I said.

Then, I saw a four-inch crystal with its glass-like pyramids poking out of the dirt.

"You brought me luck," I said and handed him the crystal.

"If you pour your energy into a crystal, your essence will be available for loved ones when you die," I said. "I mean, they'll be able to access your spirit through the crystal."

Stuart smiled at me. He held the crystal in both of his hands and then put it in his pants pocket. He kept one hand in his pocket during the rest of our walk.

He started to tell me how he met his wife at a dance. His son had been an incredible soccer player in college. I was surprised by his loquaciousness. I had thought he was a quiet man. He concluded, "If I die today, I will die a happy man."

* * *

Catherine, our guide, and the members of our group from America straggled in to the main visitor's hall for lunch. The place looked like what I had imagined, an ancient Greek Asclepius healing center, where everyone was dressed in white, milling around. Our group followed a loose schedule coming and going during the open hours at the Casa. Stuart hadn't arrived yet.

Lunch was a simple vegetarian broth prepared by volunteers. When the clinic was open, the Casa de Dom Inacio served the soup three days a week. Catherine claimed that the soup had medicinal properties. We were assured that love and saintly qualities were included in this broth.

As Stuart entered the main hall, he tripped on the wide cement step next to me and tumbled down. Blood poured from his cracked skull. People rushed to help him. As a homeopathic student, I ran to our *pousada* to get my homeopathic travel kit, which had Arnica, the remedy for bumps and bruises. I was back in less than 10 minutes.

A woman who I recognized as a doctor from George's video pronounced him dead. They had turned his body so his face was looking up at me. I opened my kit and saw the remedy Carbo vegetabilis 30c (made from vegetable charcoal). I kneeled down next to my new friend and popped the white pellets in his mouth. The remedy's keynote was to bring the dead back alive. Stuart took a breath. His eyes opened. The doctor ordered a taxi. There were no ambulances or hospitals nearby. I became part of his entourage and sat next to him, holding his hand, as he was transported to the closest medical facility 15 miles away. The doctor insisted that they send Stuart immediately to an allopathic clinic—I'm not sure why they didn't ask John of God for help.

My God! I was holding the hand of a man who had just died but was back with the living. My mind was a total blank. I entered a trance that was swept up in the chaos of the moment.

The doctor and taxi driver whisked Stuart behind closed doors. I sat in the waiting room hoping for the best. Catherine arrived and sat next to me. I told her what had happened. We held hands. The doctor came out after half an hour and told us that Stuart had died of a brain aneurysm. His son, Alec, arrived in his wheelchair. He was devastated and stared at the clinic walls. Perspiration soaked his shorts. His father had traveled so far from home for his healing—and now he was dead. How awful!

I told him to find the crystal in his father's pocket. It was meant for him. Catherine retrieved the gift and gave it to Alec, and this seemed to bring him some energy and comfort.

Catherine and Alec asked me to join them while they went to Anápolis, the closest city, to make arrangements for Stuart's body to be transported back to Edinburgh, where he could be buried with his family and friends honoring him.

At the police station, we sat through the moonless night. It took hours for the police officer on duty to ask all the necessary questions and fill out the forms. Catherine translated the questions into English so Alec could answer them and then back into Portuguese so the officer could type them on multiple carbon copies on an old-fashioned typewriter. We were the only people in the police station that night. During this somber bureaucratic procedure, I saw a gold light, the size of a basketball, up by the ceiling, in the corner of the room.

In the early morning before dawn, Alec, sitting in his wheelchair, confronted with the reality of his father's death, said to Catherine, "This must be exhausting for you. How are you?"

This golden light started to expand. I thought I was the only one who could see it. It filled the room. The warmth and love filled all our cells.

"Can you see something special?" I asked Catherine.

"Yes, of course," she said.

"It's my father," Alec said.

"It's a miracle," I said.

* * *

A few days later, my turn came for my treatment with João. I wanted to experience for myself a healing with John of God. Alex had had his healing. George was a veteran. A reporter and photographer from the major Brazillian newspaper were doing a story about the Casa that day. They took pictures of me, as I approached John of God, who was in trance. My photo was blazoned on the front page of the newspaper with the headline, "American Tourist Seeks Healing from João Teixiera de Faria," in Portuguese.

The video camera filmed me when the entity, Saint Ignatius himself, prescribed surgery. I opted for invisible surgery, of course. Unlike George, I was squeamish when it came to knives and invasive treatments.

I was escorted to a side door to John of God's right. This blue and white room was larger than the purifying and cleansing room where Alex and I had sat together for the exorcism. There were only eight people, all dressed in white, sitting on benches. I joined them. The "Ave Maria" muzak played.

We were instructed to close our eyes. I shut my eyes. A hot flash flowed through my body. Every cell tingled from the intense internal heat. I burst out in sweat that dripped on my forehead and the back of my neck. In less than 15 minutes, the invisible surgery had passed over me. I felt like I was outside of myself and my body. I shook my hands to be sure I could feel them.

I rose slowly, hardly able to walk the 20 steps out of the room. George met me on the other side of the door. I collapsed into him. He held me.

"Help me lie down," I said.

We walked slowly. I leaned on him like I had when I was in full labor with Alex, but this time I felt inhuman, separated from my body, a rag doll.

It felt like hours to reach our room in the *pousada*.

"Please leave," I said.

I didn't want anyone in the room, not George or Alex. I had to be left alone. I laid on the bed—my eyes wide open. I stared at the ceiling as it filled with pulsating balls of light. I saw all these beings surround me. They felt loving and supportive.

"You're loved for who you are, there is nothing you need to do for this love," I heard these balls of light tell me.

I understood this simple message. In my world, it was a profound confirmation. I strove to be a good person, to feel worthy of love. But I had thought I needed to earn love, and this was a mistake. This insight dropped into my core. I could take in the love, live it, and accept the part of me that had felt unlovable and separated from God.

It took several days for me to return to a new semblance of normal, to reenter the human race. I had been so sensitive to touch, to noise, to light. I had been in a cocoon until I was reborn. I entered a new chapter in my life. Now, spirit had come through the front door and was a part of me, not a guest that surprised me each time she came.

THIRD PART
PHENOMENA

"And when my fiery glance fell on the rocks, the rocks burst forth as volcanoes."

~ Hazrat Inayat Khan

CHAPTER 9
LIGHT AND DARK FORCES

"With my deep sigh the earth trembled, and when I cried aloud the name of my beloved, I shook the throne of God in heaven."

~ Hazrat Inayat Khan

We were stuck in the Brooklyn-Queens Expressway traffic. Demetra, a Greek spiritual lama from the Karma Kagyu lineage, also known as the Tibetan Buddhist Black Hatters, sat next to me, in our green Volvo. Demetra had received transmissions, direct energy, and oral teachings that acknowledged her position as a female lama, from a magical lineage founded by Milarepa, who was the Karma Kagyu's most notorious Karmapa—a Tibetan saint—whose mother had forced him to learn black magic to wreak revenge on his uncle's family. Nicholas, her ten-year-old son, sat next to Alex in the back seat of our car.

We had spent a difficult week together in our home in Bensonhurst. Alex had gone from enjoying his new playmate to being annoyed when he realized that Nicholas might be moving in. George's German sister-in-law had arranged for them to stay with us, while Demetra gave Buddhist lectures in New York City. When Demetra arrived, we found that her story was more complicated. She had left her husband and wanted a new start in America.

It was late August, 2001. George and I were doing what we could to help Demetra and Nicholas, who had the same brown eyes and curly hair as his mother, but the tensions between Nicholas and Alex had escalated. Alex piled his toys into a large mound and then threw a wooden animal or train, aiming for the older Greek boy's head. I put Alex in time out, but as soon as the four-minute timer ran out, he would run out of his bedroom, stockpile his ammunition, and start again. He had a mission to drive this boy, twenty-inches taller than him, out of his house and his life. No talking, negotiations, rewards, or punishments made a difference. We had a battle, and my son was winning. Nicholas, traumatized from his uprooting, was no match for Alex, who was aggressive and relentless. George and I had never seen this trait in our son before.

I hoped that going to Red Gables, my father's summer lake house and Zen retreat in East Brookfield, Massachusetts, might be a much needed escape for all of us, but the traffic was slowing our journey. The old Volvo had no air conditioning. Our car windows were rolled down to catch any breeze on this hot day in August. On Highway 684, a thunderstorm poured down on our car. We drove at less than 20 MPH. Although three hours into the trip, we had barely crossed the Connecticut border. Usually, we would be pulling into Red Gables' driveway by now.

"My stomach is hurting," Demetra complained. "Do you have Silica?" She had been treated by a homeopath in Athens and was asking for a remedy made from sand. Her constitutional remedy was known for treating stubbornness and digestive problems.

"No, I didn't bring my kit," I said. "Did you pack your remedy with you?" I was annoyed.

"No."

She had forgotten her remedy in Bensonhurst. The traffic dropped to 10 MPH because of flash flooding on the road. Would we ever get there?

On Highway 84 North, the traffic sped up for fifteen minutes then came to a standstill. There had been a terrible accident up ahead. Two more hours passed and progress was impossibly slow.

Demetra began to moan. She looked scared.

"What can I do for you?" I asked.

"I need a hospital," she said.

I had no idea where to find a hospital. I took the next exit and headed toward a gas station for directions. We had been in the car for six hours.

I filled the gas tank, grabbed juice boxes for the kids, water for Demetra and me, and nuts to snack on. I asked the cashier how to get to the nearest hospital. As we drove to the hospital, Demetra seemed more relaxed in anticipation of medical help.

Dark clouds gathered and blocked the setting sun. A hail storm hit us. Golf ball-sized ice balls slammed our windshield.

"This is a sign," she said. "Let's keep going to your father's home. I'm feeling better."

"It'll be past midnight by the time we get there," I told her. "Nothing will be open."

"No, I'll be OK, keep driving," she said.

I was relieved. I wanted to get out of this car. The kids had been patient, but I wasn't sure how much more they could take.

"This is so unusual," I told Demetra. "I've done this trip for years and never has anything like this happened before."

After seven-and-a-half hours, we drove down the dirt road to the Wild Goose Zendo, also known as Red Gables. A crescent moon was bright in the sky. I pulled up to the Victorian wood house with its welcoming colored stained glass window glowing in the night. I took the key hidden under a rock and opened the front door. We were safe and could rest now. The worst was behind us.

I walked into the living room and switched on the light. A black bat swooped close to my head and dive bombed at the children—frantic to find an exit. The children screamed and ran out of the house.

"Shit! Enough!" I yelled. "Demetra, you've brought these negative forces into my home, my father's house, my life. Alex was right. You must leave!"

I took a deep breath and calmed myself down. In a more relaxed tone, "Demetra, what's going on? I know you know," I said.

"Alright. I haven't told you the whole story. My rinpoche wanted me to stay in Athens," she said.

"Your spiritual teacher?" I asked.

"Yes, he didn't approve of me coming to the States—taking Nicholas with me. I disobeyed him. Now the *nāgas* are troubling us," she said.

"What are *nāgas*?" I asked.

"Serpents, unseen beings," she said.

"That's right. And you're going to take them with you! You will have to leave right away. Tomorrow, I'm driving back home. You and Nicholas need to make arrangements to go," I said.

"I'll call my travel agent in Greece. We'll get on the next flight home, as soon as we can," she said. "Nicholas is missing his father terribly, and we're running out of money."

As soon as the truth was out, her stomach pains stopped. The bat found its way out of the front door—left open for this purpose. The children came back inside. I put Alex to bed, and he fell asleep as soon as I laid him down.

Light and dark forces surrounded us. My lessons were to be in the flow, to pay attention, to be … My intuition was finding signs, synchronicities that I could follow. I had the confidence to know and accept. Alex knew, too. He had never acted in such an aggressive manner before or since. I had to trust.

* * *

A year later, on his third journey to Abadiânia, George was drawn to return to John of God's Casa de Dom Inacio. His mother had had open heart surgery that did not heal, and his father had had a stroke. He was going back to the Casa for a quick four-day trip, alone, for a long-distance healing for his parents. Alex and I hugged George goodbye on Broadway Avenue. He was taking the subway to the JFK Airport.

Our family was in transition. Cornerstone Village Cohousing was under construction—finally, we had succeeded in getting the building permits. I was driving back and forth to Cambridge to attend monthly community meetings. Alex and I stayed at my father's house in Concord, Massachusetts. Holding Alex's hand,

I walked to our old Volvo parked on West End Avenue. A tape measure fell from a seventh floor apartment and rolled under our car. I looked up, but didn't see anybody, thankful we had not been hit by this metal object.

I stopped the car to get some cash from an ATM on Broadway. I was parked illegally so I ran into the bank. I put the bank card in the machine, and the glowing green letters that appeared were not in English, but in Greek. What was going on? I had never seen Greek as an option for a language choice in any U.S. bank machine before or since.

We got on the road to drive the four hours to my father's house. I knew this car well—especially how many miles we had when the gas needle was on the eighth of a tank mark. Highway 95 North was well marked with clear signage for how many miles to the next service station. I was well within making the trip; the next rest area was 24 miles away. I came off the exit and drove down the ramp. The Volvo sputtered, skipped, and then stopped. I ran out of gas about a sixteenth of a mile from the gas station. I got out of the car. Stars and a half moon were bright on this fall night.

"Fuck! OK, enough! This is NOT funny! Tricksters, you're having too much fun at my expense. Go back to Abadiânia and play with someone else's life," I shouted at the car. Alex was asleep.

I unstrapped Alex from his car seat and carried him to the gas station. Alex jumped awake when the cold wind hit his face. He stood heroically by me, while I filled the one-gallon can. We walked back to the car, holding hands.

My relationship with entities was expanding and becoming complex. I needed to protect myself and my family from their mischief. I was learning … Thank God, those silly Abadiânia monsters left us alone forever, after that.

When George returned from the Casa, I learned that Antigone, George's mother, was helped by John of God. She had a hole in her chest from the heart surgery that wouldn't heal. When George took Antigone's picture to João, she felt dizzy more than 5,000 miles away from the healing. George heard about this synchronicity when he called his mother the next day. The Greek doctors couldn't explain how Antigone's inch-and-a-half open wound closed in a few days, after seven months of festering. George's father's health didn't improve. During the channeling, João told George he would be fine but there was not much to be done, which was God's way.

There was a spirit world I didn't understand and couldn't explain. Everything existed in an unknown reality—the good, the bad, the crazies, and those beings who just wanted to have fun!

CHAPTER 10
SUBSTANCES AND SPIRIT

"I bowed my head low in humility, and on my knees I begged of love, 'Disclose to me, I pray thee, O love, thy secret.'"

~ Hazrat Inayat Khan

I was in the ladies' bathroom, on my knees, coughing, tears streaming down my face. I had rushed out of Rose's homeopathy class because I didn't want to disrupt the class with my spasmodic cough that could last for minutes. The classroom was on the second floor in the College of Insurance, two blocks away from the World Trade Center.

The last time I'd had a cough like that was when I was an independent filmmaker, living a workaholic, childless artist's life. Rose, my homeopath, had increased my constitutional remedy Tuberculinum from a 30c to 1M (the same remedy Rose had given Alex for the first symptoms of whooping cough). My reaction had been sudden. I started to cough and cough. I was having a massive aggravation and a return of old symptoms, a clearing out of the old, a healing crisis.

But this sickness was more than I had bargained for. Tuberculinum was a miasmic remedy, based on the tubercular miasm. Dr. Samuel Hahnemann defined miasm as a taint, an infectious principle, which would predispose a person for susceptibility to a specific disease. A miasmic remedy like Tuberculinum could bring tuberculosis-like symptoms to the surface. This aggravation could be healed at the DNA level. Dr. Marvin Solit, an osteopathic doctor who studied homeopathy, explained, "Homeopathy is the only medicine that helps humans to adapt to new diseases and could assist in the evolution necessary to survive climate change."

In the distant past, my father, brother, and I had tested positive for tuberculosis in random tests. We had all had the TB vaccinations. In my early twenties, when I needed to work in a hospital for a film project, I was required to follow up the TB blood test with a chest X-ray, which fortunately showed no lesions on my lungs. I had to take Isoniazid for nine months and have monthly blood tests to check for liver toxicity. At that time, I had never had pneumonia or any upper respiratory or tuberculosis-like symptoms.

Tuberculosis, consumption, or phthisis was dubbed the White Plague. In the 19th century, it was seen as a romantic disease. During the Romanticism period, to suffer from tuberculosis represented spiritual purity and temporal wealth, an arcane idea for our times when diseases don't have cultural themes. The redemptive-spiritual perspective of the disease was made popular in modern times by films like *Les Misérables* and *Moulin Rouge*. The British poet Lord Byron wrote, "I should like to die from consumption." George Sand called her lover, Frédéric Chopin, who died young of TB, her "poor melancholy angel."

This bout of pneumonia also held potential for new opportunities. In homeopathy, "acutes" were chances for the immune system to get stronger and often would open new paths and new growths. Spiritual teacher Gurdjieff spoke about how a door, an opening never before seen, could appear and lead a person to new levels of consciousness.

Pediatricians and mothers have observed that, after a childhood acute, a child would have a leap in development. They may start to talk or walk after a fever or some other short-lived disease. At age three, after his recovery from the mumps, using homeopathy, Alex could speak full sentences.

In adults, these acutes—when not suppressed by antibiotics, cough suppressants, or pain killers—forced people to take time off and see their lives from a new perspective; they offered opportunities to make profound changes. In our culture, acutes are seen as interruptions, and the sooner one recovered, the sooner one could get back to his or her previous lives.

Nobody wants to feel ill, but the long-term costs of suppressing acutes could lead to chronic diseases. In homeopathy, symptoms are understood as the best way for the body to come back into balance. When symptoms are suppressed, the disease can sometimes go deeper to more vital organs. One example is the use of cortisone for skin eruptions. Yes, the eczema will go away, but asthma often occurs. Allopathic doctors have acknowledged the connection between eczema and asthma, but they do not always understand that the cortisone used to suppress the eczema could be causing asthma.

After I recovered from pneumonia and the Tuberculinum remedy aggravation, I wanted to start a homeopathic clinic. Emboldened by Harold, my first homeopathic teacher, and after four years of study, I felt ready to practice homeopathy; homeopaths in the United States were practicing with much less schooling and experience.

The New York State laws were explicit: It was a felony to practice medicine without a license. Fortunately, New York was not a litigious state, and homeopaths practiced with impunity under the AMA radar for decades. However, the school felt differently.

So, along with some of my classmates from homeopathy school, we rented an office for our clinic in the Lower East Side. Jennifer, the school director sent us a cease and desist letter. If we persisted with our plan, we would be expelled from the school, she wrote.

Harry, the Italian-American homeopathy student, said, "It's like telling students of a robbery school not to rob."

Two of my homeopath friends, Carol and Harry, got cold feet and dropped out of our homeopathic clinic. Marie and I brought our homeopathic services to a Brooklyn's women's shelter, where a close friend was director of the facility. We would be treating homeless women and get paid from their petty cash line item (funded by New York City tax dollars). We didn't tell Jennifer, Rose, or any other teachers at The School of Homeopathy New York.

On the first day at the women's shelter, uniformed guards searched Marie and I at the entrance. We walked through a metal detector and then found my friend, who was thrilled that we were there. She was an enlightened social service director; she had already hired other alternative health practitioners, acupuncturists, massage therapists, even life coaches for the women she cared for at the shelter.

In their assembly space that doubled as a lunch room, one of the guards had gathered a group of about 20 homeless women, mostly Latino and African Americans over 30 years old. Marie and I stood at the front of the fluorescent-lit room. Large folding tables and metal chairs filled the cafeteria, and neon hand-drawn colored posters with messages like "Believe in Yourself," "Just Say No to Drugs," and "Let's Party" were taped on the walls.

"I told the women you're here as homo therapists that give special treatments to the women, maybe lesbians," the guard said, confident in his description of homeopathy. "They will earn tokens if they show up, which they'll use for the subway, extra shampoo, or Coca-Cola."

"OK, I know you guys agreed to come here for bribes, but just to be clear, we're not here to talk about homosexuality," I said.

"I'm going to tell you about my grandmother," I said.

My grandmother was living at the Penington with her boyfriend Paul and was a walking example of the amazing healing powers of homeopathy. She was on no medications, had few ailments and lots of vital energy.

"She's 96 years old and homeopathy saved her life several times. She gets pneumonia, and when her homeopath gives her a homeopathic remedy that matches her symptoms, she gets better without going to the hospital or having to take antibiotics. The intensity and frequency of her symptoms are reduced, not just for the pneumonia but her shingles go away, even her arthritis is better."

The women were impressed with my grandmother story. They signed up for treatments immediately. And there was a waiting list.

"If she's alive, and she's that old, and this home-op thing did it, I want it too," an African American in her fifties told me.

At the shelter, I took cases that took me to the depth of human suffering. These women's stories broke my heart. Many of the women had one bad thing happen—a fire, a loss of their job, or their kid got in a gang and stole from them—and their lives spiraled out of control. They had no buffer, no support system, if things went wrong. They lived on the edge of survival. Once homeless, the climb out of this depth of poverty was often insurmountable.

The language these women used during my cases was homeopathic poetry. They had no niceties or sanitized language for what they were experiencing. Angela, a Mexican woman in her sixties, who had been a nanny for middle class white women for four decades, had recurring dreams of fires. Her actual home had burned down. Her rheumatoid arthritis felt like red hot pokers stabbing her. Her skin was chafed and raw and looked like a second degree burn. She could only need Causticum 200c (made from burnt lime with an equal amount of potassium bisulphate).

Her recovery, documented by the shelter's nurse, who dispensed our homeopathic prescriptions, was so remarkable that even the nurse wanted homeopathic treatment. Our cases were watched closely in the fishbowl-like world of administrators, social workers, therapists, nurses, and doctors. Marie and my homeopathic work came to the attention of the board of the homeless shelter. They asked us to expand our practice to the rest of their six shelters in New York City's five boroughs. We never did because I moved out of New York. Marie tried to convince the students, mostly white women and a few white men, from our homeopathy schools to work there. They told her they felt overwhelmed and under qualified for the task.

The dilemma in homeopathy was that there were few practitioners (less than two hundred certified homeopaths in the U.S. and no society that had legal power to grant government licensure). So homeopaths took great risks to practice medicine without a license. Some states were more tolerant than others. Homeopathic schools knew how hard it was for future homeopaths but didn't want the science and art to be forgotten.

Marie and I saw homeopathy working in the trenches and making a difference with seizures, AIDS, migraines, sexual abuse, schizophrenia, drug abuse, alcoholism, cancer, and Crohn's disease.

We had witnesses and the admiration of our clients, who believed in our services. They sent more and more women for homeopathic treatment. The first aphorism in Hahnemann's *Organon*: "The physician's high and only mission is to restore the sick to health, to cure, as it is termed." And I knew without a doubt that the second aphorism: "The highest ideal of a cure is rapid, gentle and permanent restoration of the health, or removal and annihilation of the disease in its whole extent, in the shortest, most reliable and most harmless way, on easily comprehensible principles," was possible.

* * *

During this busy time, Rose changed my constitutional remedy to Agaricus muscarius 200c (made from the mushroom known as toadstool or Fly Agaric fungus), another tubercular miasmic remedy. I had been well, but one persistent symptom remained uncured. I felt that I had to pee several times before I could feel my bladder empty, especially before going to bed. I never would have thought of this condition as a symptom, but now, as a homeopath in training, I paid attention to all strange, rare, and peculiar symptoms.

Agaricus was also known as the magic mushroom, the red mushroom with white dots that was featured in *Alice's Adventures in Wonderland*:

> In a minute or two the Caterpillar took the hookah out of its mouth and yawned once or twice, and shook itself. Then it got down off the mushroom and crawled away into the grass, merely remarking as it went, 'One side will make you grow taller, and the other side will make you grow shorter.' 'One side of what? The other side of what?' thought Alice to herself. 'Of the mushroom,' said the Caterpillar, just as if she had asked it aloud; and in another moment it was out of sight.

Homeopathy was also based on the Doctrine of Signatures, an old botanical theory that worked when prescribing homeopathic remedies. It was as though the remedies were archetypal and carried symbols that gave hints of their characteristics and the people who needed them. Agaricus, the mushroom, was a narcotic. The Cheshire cat told Alice, "We're mad here. I'm mad." There was a madness or "out there" quality associated with this homeopathic remedy.

Alice's willingness to drink from the bottle labeled "Poison," when she read "DRINK ME" and eat the cake that said "EAT ME," as well as her lack of hesitancy in following the rabbit down the hole, certainly confirmed the Agaricus rubrics: heedless, fearless; thoughtless, reckless, inquisitive, curious. Based on the "like cures like" principles, those rubrics did sound a lot like me so I took a dose of Agaricus, as prescribed.

At night, I dreamt I was at my own funeral. I saw George, my father, my grandmother, and Alex standing around my coffin, crying. I was there, but could not be seen. I was a ghost. The dream was so vivid it felt as if I had confronted my own death. What does it mean to be mortal? Loved and mourned?

In the dream, I felt safe in the ether, watching my body covered with soil. I sang to myself, "My baby is so fine, I'm so fine," the nursery rhyme I had made up for Alex. George and I had sang that song at his after-baptism ritual in the *aloni*, the threshing circle, in Tinos.

I lay in my own grave watching myself in the dream. I came to rest in the ground, in my grave, to be transformed and reborn in this lifetime.

Agaricus's rubric, "mind, thoughts of death," happened during that dream and afterwards. I felt it was a preparation for my future death.

When the day broke, I woke up. I felt grateful that I was alive. Cleansed, I accepted this exceptional gift of life and appreciated my life, knowing that I could die at any time. Jung had spoken in an interview shortly before his own death about how death was beyond time and space, and advised others to behave as if life was going on and on, "look forward to the next day, spend your life as if you have centuries, then you can live properly—look forward not back. Live the great adventure."

The next night, I had another death dream that shook me to my core, far worse than experiencing my own death. George was rowing in a small wooden fisherman's boat, painted in traditional Greek island blues and reds. I was with some strangers in a larger motorized tourist boat floating in the sea. I saw George's boat sink. George drowned. His straw hat floated, bobbing up and down. I grabbed his hat. The strangers told me to keep the hat as a momento of my dead husband. I woke sobbing. I was so glad to find George breathing and asleep next to me.

His love and acceptance of me had helped heal me early on in our relationship. He brought joy in everyday moments. Losing him would be devastating, far more difficult than my own death. He was part of me. Our love forged in the fires of life, I did not want to imagine his death. Not even in a dream. Goddam this remedy! Agaricus forced me to see my dependence and greatest fear. The realization loosened the grip. I saw myself letting go but hanging on, too. I was not fully ready to give him up—not to death.

This remedy also made me think of Alex—his death, a mother's worst fear. My attachments to my husband and son were tantamount to my own life. Fear of death was an attachment that some Buddhists believed could be overcome. But there was a story about a Zen monk who was weeping because his son had died. His students asked him, "Why are you crying? You're enlightened." He said, "Some attachments are more human than others." I also feared death and leaving my son motherless. However, I did feel stronger facing my fear through these dreams, reflecting on my reactions, and processing the emotions. I had more compassion for myself.

Agaricus made me explore deep-seated, unconscious parts of myself, but it did not touch my urinary symptom so Rose had an idea for a new remedy: A new classification of homeopathic mineral remedies had been discovered by Jan Scholten. He looked at the periodic table and saw each row as a stage of incarnation, beginning with Hydrogen, a remedy for people who were prone to a lack of grounding and to out of body experiences. George and Alex did well on this remedy.

The second row, Carbon remedies, was related to the birth process and people who were seeking basic needs like food and nurturing. The third row, the Natrums, dealt with issues of identity. The fourth row, the Ferrums, was about work and duty. The fifth row, the Silvers, was for artist types and homeopaths.

Rose gave me Tungsten, just left of center, Stage 6, on the sixth row, which was the Gold series for the leaders, who were focused on responsibility and power in their lives. This chart had a resemblance to the famous psychologist Erik Erikson's stage theory of psychosocial development.

Tungsten patients met challenges in their lives. They felt that they had to prove themselves as leaders in the world. Scholten explains:

> ... it is as if they are being thrown into the deep end. Now they have to learn to trust in themselves ... It is an enormous task they have taken on ... He knows he has to do it, but he doesn't know what it will be like and whether he will succeed. Like a baptism by fire. A similar situation is that of the mountain climber, who has to conquer one of the most difficult mountains with all the dangers that will entail.

Scholten's description of Tungsten continued:

> They choose the most difficult studies or the most dangerous jobs ... And when something goes wrong they'll simply try again: 'I will do it!' If you say to them 'I bet you won't dare to do that,' they'll go for it immediately ... These people are quite prepared to take on the responsibility. They like situations where they may have to save other people's lives, like firemen. Or they become mountaineers, anything where there is a challenge of life or death ... But besides the desire for a challenge there is also the fear of failure. They may have secret doubts whether they can succeed. This makes them tackle their task with great care. They may look impulsive, but this is only when the immediate situation demands such action. When they fail they feel it as a personal loss. Other people's opinions are not that important to them.

After I took Tungsten 10M (Rose continued to grow bolder with prescribing high potencies for me), I had a vision. A pen flew in front of my face with little wings. I was meant to write something but, at that time in my life, I wasn't a writer. I had no idea how fateful that image would become. Then, I heard a voice, an old man's voice talking to me. He was loquacious and kept a running monologue in my head.

"Joe needs Sulphur, Martha Natrium muriaticum," the voice prescribed remedies to people I knew.

I was channeling now. I had the awkward feeling that Pat Rodegast must have experienced with Emmanuel rumbling in her head. I even had a taste of what John of God goes through when Dom Inacio takes over his body. I was me, but I was sharing myself with someone else. What or who was this entity?

"Who are you?" I asked the voice in my head.

"I'm Allen," he said.

I was channeling the famous Henry Clay Allen, who wrote one of the most comprehensive Materia Medica books.

"No," he said in my head. "I'm the other Allen. Go to your book shelf, take down *The Faces of Homeopathy* book, go to page 240. I'm the man in the photo in the first row, three in from the right."

In the book, on the page he indicated, I found J. H. Allen's photograph standing in a suit and straw hat next to 40 other American homeopaths. I looked him up. He had written *The Chronic Miasms, I & II*, which I had never heard of before.

At night, while bathing in hot water, I noticed a vertical white line in the middle of my right big toe. Shamans believe that such lines are a sign of a kundalini rising; the uncoiling of the two serpents at the base of the spine, rising up to the middle of the forehead in the third eye area is the metaphor for this spiritual awakening.

Could I trust this voice? Did this downloaded knowledge bring wisdom? I would learn from Allen, follow his work, and understand more and more how Akashic records—information encoded in a non-physical plane of existence—could be accessed through other realms, something George had been fascinated by and explored for years.

There was a physical aspect to Tungsten, as well. My appetite changed. Before taking the remedy, I would finish a meal and be ready for more. No matter how much I ate, I was always longing for more. Now, I wasn't hungry all the time. The insatiable hunger I had felt since I was a teenager disappeared. I finally felt satiated and nourished.

After taking Tungsten, I also had the urge to throw out all my journals (a mixture of business and personal writing—descriptions of dreams, random thoughts, grocery lists, to dos, etc.). I gave my feminist, diet, and spiritual books to the local library to make room for the new in my life. Remedies initiated purges, examinations of beliefs, letting go of fears. When I was seeing patients in their homes, I once told a client who had AIDS how I believed homeopathy sped up evolution. He looked at me aghast.

"So I'll die sooner," he said.

That was not what I meant. I saw homeopathy as jump starting new directions in our lives. It was similar to the way George began a new destiny when he developed a new hara line (as Traci called the vertical energetic core) after John of God scraped his eyes. After homeopathy, I took on unforeseeable challenges, opened myself up for the greatest of breakthroughs, and lived to answer my biggest question: how to be in the here and now.

As an eclectic spiritual practitioner, starting with Gurdjieff's teachings based on Sufism and Buddhist practices, I revisited teachings that were foundational for me to grow. Hazrat Inayat Khan, a Sufi teacher from India, wrote a poem, "The Dance of the Soul," that said it most eloquently:

> I have loved in life and I have been loved.
>
> I have drunk the bowl of poison from the hands of love as nectar, and have been raised above life's joy and sorrow.
>
> My heart, aflame in love, set afire every heart that came in touch with it.
>
> My heart has been rent and joined again;
>
> My heart has been broken and again made whole;
>
> My heart has been wounded and healed again;
>
> A thousand deaths my heart has died, and thanks

be to love, it lives yet.

I went through hell and saw there love's raging fire, and I entered heaven illumined with the light of love.

I wept in love and made all weep with me;

I mourned in love and pierced the hearts of men;

And when my fiery glance fell on the rocks, the rocks burst forth as volcanoes.

The whole world sank in the flood caused by my one tear;

With my deep sigh the earth trembled, and when I cried aloud the name of my beloved,

I shook the throne of God in heaven.

I bowed my head low in humility, and on my knees I begged of love, "Disclose to me, I pray thee, O love, thy secret."

She took me gently by my arms and lifted me above the earth, and spoke softly in my ear, "My dear one, thou thyself art love, art lover, and thyself art the beloved whom thou hast adored."

My soul held the feelings, the fears, the grief, the pains, and the intensity of love I knew as a mother, healer, and lover. I learned to stay open to the moments of life, whatever they may bring ... My body was the vessel for the intensity of life, the journey and instrument for carrying the transformation.

CHAPTER 11
CALAMITY

"She took me gently by my arms and lifted me above the earth, and spoke softly in my ear, 'My dear one, though thyself art love, art lover, and thyself art the beloved whom thou hast adored.'"

~ Hazrat Inayat Khan

"Can you take me home? Paul is waiting for me at the Penington," my grandmother said. She paced at the top of the stairs of our second floor apartment in Bensenhurst, Brooklyn, all ready to go in her ivory cashmere coat and perfectly applied, Marilyn Monroe red lipstick.

"Wait a sec while I get Baby Love in his carrier," I said.

"Grandmom, look at my train. It's Thomas," four-year-old Alex said. "See, it's blue."

My grandmother had spent the long weekend with us because her aide had taken some time off.

I strapped Alex into his booster seat next to Baby Love, who meowed in his carrier. My grandmother seat-belted herself next to me in the green Volvo.

"You can't go anywhere," shouted the Italian-American landlady, running out of her basement apartment onto the street where we were parked.

"What?" I said.

"There's a war. An airplane hit the World Trade Center. Go inside now. Protect yourselves. You can watch everything on TV," she said.

"Oh, dear," my grandmother said. "We're all going to die. Baby Love, where are you?"

"Grandmom, nobody's going to die," I said.

"War!" yelled Alex and made gunfire sounds.

I unstrapped Alex and lifted him on my hip to carry him inside. My grandmother held my elbow. We entered our quiet apartment. I turned on the TV. Footage broadcasted of the Boeing 767 jumbo jet hitting the first tower. White billows of smoke poured out of the tower's gaping hole. The news commentator shouted, "There's another plane approaching."

Alex was playing with his Thomas train set, oblivious to what was on the TV. My grandmother started to look for Baby Love, whom I had forgotten in the car. I watched on TV as United Airlines flight #175 from Boston hit the second tower.

"A passenger plane flew into the 81st floor of the World Trade Center," the reporter said, as sirens blasted in the background. Then, the inevitable happened. One after the other, the floors disappeared into clouds of dust, until both towers collapsed onto themselves into war zone-like rubble, killing thousands of people.

Three days before, I had been in a homeopathy class, a block away from Ground Zero. Today, we could have been trapped in the Battery tunnel, a few blocks from the towers.

"Baby Love! Where is Baby Love?" I heard my grandmother asking for her cat.

"Oh, I'm sorry grandmom," I said. I ran back to our car parked in front of the house and grabbed the cat carrier with Baby Love in it.

The landlady had gotten it wrong. We were not at war, not yet. In 1982, I had been a war journalist in Afghanistan for CBS and the BBC during the Soviet occupation.

This violence, 9/11, and the wars that raged afterwards, rose from the ashes of centuries of ignorance, intolerance, brutality, and male dominance. Patriarchy, often times advanced in religious institutions, betrayed the healthy male and female principles in each of us. It sought to have control over others in the name of God.

In my twenties, I grappled with the male and female polarities. I experienced the male energy as goal-oriented, heroic, and visionary, while the female energy was nurturing, intuitive, and receptive. Then, I discovered a healthy expression of both aspects of myself, which emerged as a creative endeavor, when I produced *Women in Limbo Presents*. The limbo representing the in-between stage of existence and balancing both the feminine and male principles in myself.

This terrorist attack was a symptom of the collective, not an isolated event, but representative of centuries of separation from nature, from the collective self, from the care of all sentient beings, humans, animals, plants, minerals, the seen, and the unseen. Jung wrote about the split between spirit and matter, which needed to be resolved through the unconscious. Matter must be recognized as an aspect of the Great Mother, the Divine Feminine—our soul interconnected with matter. Elizabeth Lesser wrote, "And when human reason becomes the dominating force ... patriarchal culture then excuses its excesses—war, greed, exploitation—as normal and natural, as the way it just *is*."

* * *

Marie and I were on the phone. Our families were in the city. George was working in the A.C.L.U. office near Battery Park. He made it home on the subway, before they closed down all the trains.

Marie's youngest son, David, was in third grade at the Charter public school, a few blocks from the Twin Towers. Her older son was in Queens and in no danger. Pedro, Marie's husband, rode his bike across the Williamsburg Bridge to rescue his son. They rode together, with David sitting on the metal rack over the back wheel.

"I saw people jump from the World Trade Center. They must have killed themselves," David said.

We both stayed on the phone, a lifeline connection until her two sons and our husbands were home. During these waiting hours, we made a plan.

"This cannot be happening," Marie said.

"I can't watch anymore—those planes, those people ... I have to turn it off," I said.

"What about our CHC exam? We're supposed to take the test on Saturday," she said.

"I don't know. We've been studying this homeopathy stuff for months. Do you think it will happen?" I asked.

"Maybe. We can't give up now," she said.

I wasn't so sure my certification to be a homeopath mattered anymore. Marie would come over to our place, and we would do a final cram session. George would take Alex and my grandmother to Marie's house. The two fathers would take care of the families there, while we went into retreat preparing to become certified homeopaths.

Marie moved in for four days, as we prepared for the final eight-hour exam. It would take place at the Penington and be supervised by Samantha, the manager. We turned off all news about 9/11 and studied the Materia Medica, taking sample cases and talking on and on about miasms.

"9/11 is the Syphilitic miasm," I said. I wanted to make sense of what had happened.

"Syphilitic miasm has that do or die attitude. My way or the highway," she said.

"Hahnemann discovered miasms to make sense of disease," I said.

"He was searching for the source of disease, not just its current manifestations," said Marie, quoting from her study notes. "James Kent called miasms a spiritual sickness." Kent was an American homeopath during the early twentieth century who had a major impact on homeopathy worldwide.

"What do you think he meant?" I asked.

"Well Psora, the first miasm—"

"Came from scabies, those awful pustules, erupting on the skin," I said. "This first disease, Kent said, was the punishment for Eve taking the apple from the snake, expulsion from the Garden of Eden"

"Original sin, Dr. Kent's Christian Swedenborg beliefs

imposed on Hahnemann's root cause of disease," she said. "More important was the recognition that disease was an imbalance of the internal not external."

"Still, a radical belief that the imbalance of the vital force—prana, chi—was the cause of disease, not some outside agent," I said.

"How do you think he explained poisons, epidemics, and accidents?" she asked.

"There is susceptibility and karma. No accidents really. Everything happens for a purpose," I said.

"Really, is there anything good that can come from 9/11?" My best friend, the devil's advocate, made me go deeper, asking the hardest questions.

"My understanding is that the vital force is our collective consciousness, emanating in everything—our soul evolving. Miasms are the morphic fields that crisscross our human experiences. A true cure exists through recognizing miasms and healing the vital force, beyond time and space," I said.

"Miasms are related to infectious diseases, handed down to descendants, genetic perhaps through the DNA, but morphic fields—what are you talking about?" she asked.

"Ancient diseases. Ways of thinking. Matrixes were imprinted and left a stain, which is passed down to modern times. These blockages, taints, or stains are carried invisibly, drain our energies, and generate symptoms: diseases at a personal and collective level," I said, making it up as I went.

"Miasms and vital force are together in a mystical union. I see the healing of ourselves, our planet, and the universe coming from this deep awareness that consciousness permeates everything. Nurturing all is more important than conquering nature. Fighting diseases with force and invasive treatments doesn't bring health and wellbeing," I preached to my dearest friend, who shared my passion for homeopathy and spiritual explorations.

* * *

In the aftermath of 9/11, the Council for Homeopathic Certification exam was postponed for two weeks, until Federal Express could deliver the exams to the manager at the Penington. My Abadiânia photographic memory had been dislodged by all the events. I failed the exam by a point. My friend passed with high marks.

Marie and I had clung to each other in our homeopathic bubble, keeping the real world at the periphery during this national tragedy, before taking the exam. When we emerged, we were stunned by the altars placed all over the city, candles on the sidewalks burning for loved ones, faded flowers laid next to Teddy Bears, cut-out pink paper hearts, and photographs of New Yorkers who had died. I felt love emanating from the city. The spirits of the deceased blessed us, the survivors. I felt a surreal calmness in the weeks after 9/11.

CHAPTER 12

AUROVILLE

"In everything, everywhere, in all relations truth must be brought out in its all-embracing rhythm and every movement of life should be an expression of beauty and harmony."

~ The Mother, founder of Auroville

I wheeled my compact red suitcase to the curb outside Chennai airport in southeast India. At 3 a.m., the hot humid wall of activity was palpable. Yellow and green rickshaws, hawking vendor in cotton tunics and pantaloons, and taxi drivers waving from their black and white 1950s curvy cabs assaulted me. I had flown from New York City for more than 18 hours to get to my destination.

I had left home the day after Thanksgiving, on my 40th birthday, two-and-a-half months after 9/11. My family forgot my birthday (except George, who brought me roses and a card in the morning). We were at my father's Concord house, enacting a similar scene from the Thanksgiving when I had fought with my father over vaccinating Alex. The traditional turkey dinner, mashed potatoes, cranberry sauce, and pumpkin pie were served in the womb-like dining room.

"Bomb Al-Qaeda. It'll be a quick war, in and out. We'll show them. Don't mess with Americans," my brother, the medical student, said.

"There are no quick wars—those mountains are impenetrable. The British couldn't beat the Afghans, nor the Soviets. This is ridiculous," I said.

"They'll find Osama Bin Laden," my father said.

"Iraq will be next. We'll just take their oil, we deserve the bounty," my brother said.

"The rest of the world will just hate us, worse than colonialists," I said. "Don't trust everything you hear in the news. There are no easy ways to get out of a war. Remember Vietnam."

"You just don't get it," my brother said. "Your anti-war stance makes you such a wimp."

"May I remind you, I was a war journalist in AFGHANISTAN. Who are you to call me a wimp?" I was angry. "I'm going to India tomorrow, and it will not be soon enough to get out of this war-mongering country."

Outside of the Chennai airport, a young boy grabbed my suitcase out of my hand, and I had to follow him. He put the suitcase in the open trunk. This would be my taxi. I climbed in the back and told the driver my destination, the Park Guest House in Auroville. The taxi driver waved his head side to side, the Indian "yes" gesture.

Since I was a kid, I had thought that I would go to India when I turned 40. It was an idea that had been planted in my mind for nearly three decades, and now it was being harvested. I would be gone for 40 days on a quest. George agreed to stay behind and take care of Alex and my grandmother, who was still living at the Penington. I arranged for babysitters while he worked at the A.C.L.U. and a second aide to look after my grandmother on the weekends.

My plan was to stay a week in Auroville. My friend, who was a devotee of Sri Aurobindo and Mirra Alfassa, a mystic called The Mother, insisted that I begin my travels in this intentional spiritual community. She had two life-sized black and white photographs behind her altar in her Brooklyn loft. The Mother, a French-Turkish lady in her 80s, sat in a wooden carved chair and looked a lot like my grandmother with her wide, vibrant eyes. Sri Aurobindo, an elderly white-bearded Indian man in a white toga-like cloth, sat on a modern throne that made him look like Zeus.

My plan was to spend a week in Auroville in Tamil Nadu, then to go to Mumbai and work on cataloguing video cases taken by Dr. Jayesh Shah, an internationally acclaimed Indian homeopath, My friend Marie asked me if I wanted to take one of her orchid flower essences to set an intention for this epic journey. With my eyes closed, as instructed, I picked a bottle out of the box. The label was in Spanish so my friend translated. "Standing Still," she read. How odd? I was going to travel thousands of miles and stand still.

I took the few pellets—similar to homeopathic remedies in that they are highly diluted substances but they are meant for emotional support or meditational purposes. Bach Flower Remedies were the most well-known flower essences. Rescue Remedy was my go-to flower essence for my grandmother, when her anxiety was at its peak.

In the taxi, with the windows rolled down, I watched the trucks sandwiched close to us and the motorbikes in the breakdown lane. We were driving like the English, on the opposite side of the road. Rain poured down hard in this monsoon season. The driver leaned his left arm out of the window to brush the rain off the windshield, to see the road ahead; he didn't have any windshield wipers.

I leaned back on the well-worn black leather seat. Its cracks and rips looked like they had been there for at least a decade. My senses heightened, I inhaled jasmine. I could not understand how there could be so many jasmine trees in India. In Pyrgos, George's family village in Tinos, the same scent was present everywhere at night. How could it be possible to smell this most intoxicating flower as we drove through Tamil Nadu?

After several hours, the traffic died down and the sun rose. The torrential rain stopped. We were in the countryside of one of the poorest regions in India. I saw salt mounds on the banks of still waters. Rice paddies, where large oxen chewed on grass, were flooded. Then, we turned right at a hand-painted wooden sign that said "Auroville," and up the hill we drove. Lush banyan trees grew by the side of the road. Westerners dressed like Indians, in bright pink, yellow, and green Punjabi cotton clothes, passed by. We toured around and around, the roads were circular like a beltway. First, we went counterclockwise, then clockwise, reading all the guesthouse signs. After 45 minutes of touring, still fully alert after more than 40 hours, with no sleep, I asked a French lady where we could find the Park Guest House.

"Madam, no such guest house here. You must mean the Ashram guest house in Pondicherry by the ocean," she said.

My taxi driver looked at me.

"I'm so sorry," I told the driver. "I'll pay more. It's all my fault."

The left right shake of his head indicated he was OK with this solution. We drove back down to the main road and another half hour on a trafficked street—motorbikes with both parents and three kids riding on the back, busses blaring Bollywood songs, oxen with their painted and decorated horns, and children darting in and out through the puddles.

We drove along a beach with the Indian Ocean splashing on the shore to Pondicherry. On a metal sign, next to an iron gate, the letters, "Park Guest House," were painted in pink. We had arrived. My body finally registered the hours of travel. As the driver handed me my suitcase and I paid him in rupees, I spotted a garland of jasmine hanging from his taxi rear view mirror. We had carried the scent with us all night long.

I slept all day. My day-for-night turned backwards from the jet lag and 11-hour time difference. On the second day, when I awoke and the manager's office was open, I asked about where to stay in Auroville. I took a rickshaw, which roared its way to the Centre Guest house, at the epicenter of Auroville.

Auroville was meant to be a universal town, where men and women of all countries could live in peace and harmony, beyond creeds, politics, and nationalities. The purpose of Auroville was to realize human unity. The Mother, the founder of Auroville, wrote her dream, which has been published widely:

> There should be somewhere on earth a place, which no nation could claim as its own, where all human beings of goodwill who have a sincere aspiration could live freely as citizens of the world and obey one single authority, that of the supreme Truth; a place of peace, concord and harmony where all the

fighting instincts of man would be used exclusively to conquer the causes of his sufferings and miseries, to surmount his weaknesses and ignorance, to triumph over his limitations and incapacities; a place where the needs of the spirit and the concern for progress would take precedence over the satisfaction of desires and passions, the search for pleasure and material enjoyment.

I checked into a modern two-room cement building. My suite had a 14-foot ceiling, a wax-polished red cement floor, air conditioning, and a tiled bathroom with a shower and Western toilet. I bought dozens of books at the Auroville Visitor Centre's bookstore and spent several days reading all the literature available on Auroville, The Mother, and Sri Aurobindo. The books were printed on thin rice-like paper, which reminded me of all the homeopathy books I had read that had been printed in India.

My world was shifting, cracking open. I was assimilating ideas, and I was standing still. For days, I didn't leave that small building at the Centre Guest House—except for meals under the Banyan tree. I cancelled my trip to Mumbai. I would not leave Auroville. Something was pulling me to stay put, not explore; my usual tubercular miasm was turned down. I rented a moped and, when I wasn't reading, I drove the red dirt roads, drinking in some kind of nourishment that I had lacked. It was like I had lived my whole life in a desert, and now there was plenty of water. I drank the earth here, its essence. I found something I had never experienced before. Auroville filled me like sunshine, as when George and I vacationed in Tinos and returned to Manhattan with recharged batteries, except this essence came from the earth, not from holiday rest, sea, and sunshine. It was as though India provided me with a missing basic nutrient.

In the texts, biographies of The Mother and Sri Aurobindo, I glimpsed an integrity of ideas. In my life, I had separated religion, spirituality, medicine, homeopathy, motherhood, wifehood, family, and community as compartments to be managed. It was like a pie with sections, and I would give each one my time and resources in a clockwork fashion.

Now, I followed the rhythms of the day—leaning in to what was needed in the moment, less concerned with reaching individual goals, more in the flow.

The image of Sri Aurobindo's symbol, two triangles facing upward and downward, like the star of David, crystallized what I was feeling about integrating spirit and matter. Inside the triangles, a square is drawn inside the junction. Inside the square, a lotus floating on water is the symbol of matter. Sri Aurobindo wrote, "the Divine Consciousness manifesting itself at last here in this very realm of Matter, and transforming the physical body in its divinized form to come."

The Mother's original name was Mirra Alfassa, and she had her own symbol, a central circle that represented the Divine Consciousness (an evolutionary force). The four petals represented her four powers: Maheshwari for compassion, Mahakali for passion, Mahalakshmi for beauty and harmony, and Mahasaraswati for knowledge.

The twelve petals represented her twelve virtues that manifested for Her work: sincerity, peace, equality, generosity, goodness, courage, progress, receptivity, aspiration, perseverance, gratitude, and humility. Now that was some symbol to honor a living and breathing woman! Give me the circle, four petals, and twelve petals instead of the Christian cross any day!

* * *

At sunrise, I walked through Auroville's Matrimandir, known as the Soul of the City. The monsoon rains had taken a few days off. Mist rose up from the red dirt. I visited the sacred garden, which was landscaped to represent The Mother's twelve consciousnesses: Existence, Consciousness, Bliss, Light, Life, Power, Wealth, Utility, Progress, Youth, Harmony, Perfection.

In flip-flops and wearing a light yellow Punjabi garment, I walked through the Garden of Existence, planted with pink hibiscus to remind visitors of psychic aspiration. At the Garden of Wealth, water lilies exposed their yellow and magenta stamens in ponds. The Mother said the garden would be a place where "One must know how to move from consciousness to consciousness."

In the center of the garden, the golden Matrimandir grew out of the ground, a UFO-like, globe shaped building. I showed my guest pass to the Aurovillian, whose work was to welcome and check guests who entered the meditation hall. I climbed the under-construction, spaceship-like ramp and walked up to the double door, where I left my flip-flops. Another Aurovillian handed me white socks to put on. Inside, the foggy, air-conditioned interior felt peaceful and still.

The domed round room was pure white, with 12 columns over 50 feet high, white marble floors and walls, and white cushions. A hole in the ceiling brought a shaft of light, a beam that struck a three-foot, clear crystal ball, refracting rainbows throughout the inner chamber. Over a hundred meditators could fit in this sanctuary, but this early in the morning there were less than a dozen of us.

On the cushion, cross-legged, I dropped into a vast open space. Decades of meditation practice helped my mind to quiet quickly. The experience of turning 40, my readings, contemplations, and the abundance of Aurovillian and Indian essence swelled in me. I felt a stirring at the base of my spine. A pulsation moved up through to the top of my head. My crown felt tingly. I rocked forward and backward as this charge surged through me, causing orgasmic contractions in my vagina. My body pulsated. Particles of me dispersed and blended with particles of the Matrimandir, Mother Earth, and the Cosmos. I had become one with All, in this shrine dedicated to the Universal Mother.

* * *

A few days after my kundalini rising experience, I sat under the banyan tree at the Centre Guest House eating dal, rice, and pickled chutneys. Isabelle, the assistant manager, a French woman with a soft voice, said she was leaving the next day for a 10-day Vipassana meditation at Goenka's Chennai retreat center.

"Would you like to join me?" she asked.

"Do you think I could sit on a chair?" I asked, thinking this would make the retreat easier and more bearable.

"*Mais bien, sûr*. It's not about the form. It's about the discovery," she said.

"Are you sure I can get a chair?" I asked again. I did not want to sit cross-legged on a cushion on the floor for the 11 hours of meditation a day.

"You ask the teacher on the first day," she said. "She'll give you a chair."

Zen sesshin, a meditation retreat, followed a warrior-like boot camp schedule. I wanted to avoid the excruciating pain in my knees and long hours culminating in an all-night sitting session on the floor. This Vipassana retreat sounded like a good compromise.

"I'll come with you," I decided.

We headed off at daybreak in one of the black and white taxis with the jasmine garland hanging from the rear view mirror. The monsoon rains pitted the road so we had to swerve around craters that could swallow the taxi whole. When we arrived at the retreat center in the suburbs of Chennai, the women's halls, separated from the men's dormitory, were not full. Isabelle and I would each get our own private room, a cement cell, a single bed in an otherwise empty room, and a private bathroom with an Indian style toilet (a hole in the floor), and a shower. I was grateful. There were no charges for the retreat, food, or accommodation—everything was paid for by voluntary contributions.

At the orientation in the evening, we were instructed to keep our eyes to the ground at all times and do absolutely no talking. The middle-aged male teacher sat in full lotus position (cross-legged with his ankles pulled under his knees) on the left side of the room, where the men sat in neat rows. A five-foot aisle separated the men's side from the women's side. An elderly woman teacher with grey hair sat on a single cushion also in full lotus. She told anyone who had a question to visit her room after this meeting.

I found her room. Her assistant ushered me in. The teacher sat in lotus on a wooden platform-like chair.

"I heard that it's possible to have a chair for meditation," I said.

"Do you have any health reasons for this request?" she asked.

"No," I answered too quickly.

"No chair. Take cushions like rest of Vipassana meditators," she said.

In that instant, my attachment to comfort—a chair, things I could control—was evaporated by her words. I felt no resistance to her demand.

For 10 days I sat on cushions, and my knees did hurt. I could move my legs—unlike the Zen rules that chastised for fidgeting or adjusting the posture. In Zen, the sittings were no longer than 45 minutes and were followed by an ambulatory meditation, during which I could walk and work out the stiffness and any joint pains. But here in Goenka's Vipassana retreats, I crawled to my room and collapsed, exhausted from the ninety-minute or longer meditations. Only after lunch, when we had a three-hour break, would I walk the walkway with the other women. The monsoon downpours and huge puddles kept us out of the garden.

Goenka's videotaped voice gave us instructions at night on how to meditate. These were not so different from the Gurdjieff meditations I knew. Eyes were kept closed, as I followed the breath in my body. Goenka promised each day that he would give us new instructions that would bring us closer to clearing out sankharas—karma—and release us from the countless cycles of life, death, and rebirth.

"*Aneka jati samsaram,*" Goenka boomed from the video.

Our meditations were meant to destroy old karma and prevent us from creating new ones in this lifetime. We would achieve a state of total liberation and enlightenment, the ultimate victory of light over darkness, if we kept meditating.

* * *

I waited for the final instruction on the fourth day, and found myself observing the sensations of my body from head to toe, through my right shoulder down to my fingers, then down my right side of the body, down to my toes. I was aware of the pulsation of every cell in my body, tracked in each breath, minute by minute, for hours at a time, and days going by.

I felt myself in my body and a part of All, at the same time.

This was a new sensation and realization that became an ongoing experience—not the flash of ecstatic bliss I had experienced in the Matrimandir and in Afghanistan. I felt I was bringing consciousness into matter, into my own body, as described by Sri Aurobindo. This life force that connected all of life could be experiential and palpable at any moment, by tuning in to the breath and the sensations in the body.

With three days left in the Vipassana, I took a new direction, no longer following Goenka's nightly instructions. I sat in the pulsation that I was able to access all the time. I visualized each organ in my body, which I could imagine based on the dissection course I had taken the year before.

The toxic, formaldehyde-soaked corpse that I had dissected was a 57-year-old tattooed women who had died from cirrhosis of the liver; the coincidence was not missed. This woman had died at that same age as my mother and of the same cause. I opened her with a sharp pen knife, unpeeling the skin, removing the thick layers of spongy fascia, to the thin casing around her precious liver, heart, stomach, lungs: another world revealed through meticulous work and fearlessness. I was reverent toward this woman who donated her body to science and bared her physical self for me to explore like a spelunker. I had flashes of insights and images. I saw a cottage near the bank of a river. I couldn't prove that what I saw was her memories, but I felt sadness at times, rage at other moments. I also felt love, deep love, as I took each organ out of her body, with the help of the instructor, and placed them on a metal gurney. I was in awe of the human, our parts and our vulnerability.

Then, on the final two days of the Vipassana meditation retreat, I reviewed my life as far back as I could remember. I started with my birth, revisiting the images I had experienced in a past life regression conducted by a student of Dr. Roger Woolger, a British-American psychotherapist. I saw myself carried by two Renaissance angels, while my mother was passed out on the hospital bed. Then, the nurse took me to my mother. The pearly angels lifted my drugged-out mother from the painkillers, commonly prescribed to women giving birth in the 60s. I saw her smile, and breast-feed me. I later found a photo of her holding my newborn self in her arms, asleep with a beatific smile on her angel face. I was a loved baby.

Then I saw my teenage years, awkward, fat but inspired to write plays, direct them, make Super 8 films. I would tell my family story through regal myths: my mother was Queen Elizabeth, my father Sir Charles. My mother congratulating me on the play, not realizing the lead woman who ordered everyone around, "I am the queen. Do as I say," was based on her.

With the sensations pulsating through my body, I revisited my first kiss with George sitting on his couch, in front of a coin-operated TV in an East London house. We cuddled on his single bed. I refused to make love to him because he had invited a homeless friend of his to sleep on the floor in his bedroom. Then, we made love the next day in my pension room in Bayswater, after we ate purple chicken that I had made on a one-burner gas plate. The raspberry sauce turned blueberry purple when I added cream.

Each major moment of my life was revisited: my mother's funeral, throwing her ashes on the Arizona mountaintop, honoring her passing.

* * *

When I returned home from India, I felt the blast of cold opening the refrigerator door, the heat of the flame on the gas stove, heard my son's giggles, saw the light shaft stream through the kitchen window as I made lunch for Alex. All the cells in my body were absorbing nutrients from this daily life experience. I was nourished by all the senses.

After the Vipassana retreat, the observer in me followed my sensations, pulsations that vibrated through me and through everything around me. The spirit of unrealities and the soul of matter, male and female energies combined to BE, the I AM, the awakening. My striving left behind at Abadiânia, the Zen discipline replaced with a softer meditation that I could practice all the time—awake, following my breath—no need or desire to run off to a cave to reach enlightenment. This pulsation was the life blood of LIFE, GOD, GODDESS, REALITY!

EPILOGUE
MYSTERY

"Magic teaches us to create portals, to open doors and dare the wilderness."

~ Starhawk

In 2002, George, Alex, and I, along with my grandmother, moved to Cambridge, into a duplex apartment at Cornerstone Village Cohousing. Paul's epileptic seizures had become more frequent and more intense, scaring the Penington residents. His sudden falls and convulsions were too much for the little peace of Manhattan. His children arrived and moved him to Buffalo.

I painted the walls of our new duplex apartment with pigment paints in swift motions, burnt sienna, cobalt blue, cadmium red, and milk white. I felt like a painter splashing earth's richness in our mammal's den. I feng shuied each object, infusing intentions for our wealth corner, relationship corner, ancestors corner, etc. I placed my altar in the good fortune center with pictures of The Mother, Sri Aurobindo, George, and Alex, the spirit, soul, and beings in my life who I honored more than anything.

George left his job at the A.C.L.U. and became my business manager for Inner Health, our new homeopathic clinic in Cambridge, while I treated the patients. Alex began kindergarten at the nearby Waldorf School of Lexington. My father's company sold, and he was very generous with his stocks. George and I were provided with a new wealth we had never experienced before.

My father invited us to Dai Bosatsu Dojo in the Catskills for his roshi ordination. He was becoming a bishop in his Zen community. George drove Alex and me through the winding valley, where a crick gushed over ancient rocks, until we arrived at the Japanese curved roof temple of the Zen monastery. We sat as the incense was lit. My father's head was shaved in front of us. He was dressed in custom-made silk robes from Japan for the occasion—medallions, similar to The Mother's four petal symbol, were woven in his garment. My father, now called Dai Fu, was to receive a transmission from his teacher that had been passed down through chanted memories for centuries in the Mahayana tradition: the Heart sutra, form is emptiness and emptiness is form.

The gongs rang. The Japanese prayers chanted. My father bowed to his teacher. Women were not allowed to receive these sacraments in this tradition, but I had embodied them in my own eclectic spiritual journey through homeopathy, spirituality, shamanic experiences, motherhood, wifehood, daughterhood, and granddaughterhood. These were the meanings of a life well lived.

The Mother of Auroville, my role model, who was a successful entrepreneur, founded over 300 thriving small businesses in Pondicherry, ran the largest ashram, created an intentional town dedicated to peace and global harmony, and lived spirit and soul together in one body. She was not afraid of phenomena and reality coexisting. And neither was I.

I took my ongoing pulsating reality and lived moment by moment. A rebirth, a simplified existence, and yet a level of wisdom honors me day in and day out.

ACKNOWLEDGEMENTS

Yearning for Magic is my second memoir, the one I had envisioned writing first. Instead, *My Journey Through War and Peace* poured out of me, the stories of my twenties. Now, I understand how I needed my writing supporters, some experience with writing memoirs, and lots of encouragement to tackle the stories of my thirties.

The friends who believed in me and supported me are Kate Soudant, Julie Matthaei, Dawn Jordan, Gloria Rossi-Menedes, Natasha Charles, and Jean LeVaux. GrubStreet continues to be my home of writers, which I'm happy I found when I was writing my first memoir. Family members—George, Alex, Elena, Leslie, Dad—were cheerleaders all the way.

My editor, Arlinda Shtuni stepped in and offered her magic to make the book more cohesive. David Yeager copyedited, cleaned up grammatical errors, and fact checked.

Cornerstone Cohousing Village offered a safe haven to write. Turkey Land Cove Foundation offered that room of one's own, which actually was a whole house, to complete the final draft. My Gaia Press team, Martha Bullen, Alexandra Honeysett, Tracy Grigoriades, Dan Be Kim, Brigid Gorry-Hines, and Eva Case-Issakov, gave me the support to publish this book.

I'm grateful to all my homeopathic friends, mentors, and colleagues (you know who you are) for practicing homeopathy and making the community stronger.

My many thanks to you all, family, friends, and colleagues, for your support, love, and friendship. All of you contributed in some way to make this book possible. I am eternally grateful!

~ Melissa

ABOUT THE AUTHOR

Melissa Burch is a bestselling author, teacher and speaker who inspires men and women to explore and develop their own spiritual practices rooted in the teachings of the heroine's journey. A lifelong explorer of both the internal and external, Melissa's first career was as a filmmaker, producer and former war journalist for the BBC, CBS, and other networks. She was just in her twenties when she traveled with the mujahedeen, filmed an attack on a Soviet convoy, slept with an Afghan commander, and climbed 14,000 foot mountains in the Hindu Kush. These experiences and many more are featured in her first memoir, *My Journey Through War and Peace: Explorations of a Young Filmmaker, Feminist and Spiritual Seeker*.

Melissa also spent many years as the executive producer of *Women in Limbo Presents*, a national public television series that featured edgy, raw and profoundly human stories about women's lives, and served as president of the New York Film/Video Council.

In the next iteration of her own heroine's journey, Melissa spent several years as an internationally recognized leader in homeopathy, co-founded the Catalyst School of Homeopathy and produced and hosted one of the first successful radio shows on Voice America on homeopathy.

In addition to what will be her three-part memoir, Melissa is also the author of the bestseller *The Four Methods of Journal Writing: Finding Yourself Through Memoir*.

Melissa, and her husband and her college-bound son recently completed a three month 16-city book tour, which they called "The Heroine's Journey: Road Trip and Quest" across the United States.

You can learn more about Melissa and sign-up to read her blog and insights on exploring and developing your own spiritual practice at www.melissa-burch.com.

DISCOVER MORE ABOUT *YEARNING FOR MAGIC* AND *THE HEROINE'S JOURNEY*

Visit the author's website, www.melissa-burch.com, for more information on upcoming events, blogs and ways to enter the conversation on spirituality, adventure, holistic health, and memoirs.

Get your free Heroine's Journey Workbook to join her in an adventurous life at melissa-burch.com/heroinesjourneyworkbook-ebook.

www.ingramcontent.com/pod-product-compliance
Lightning Source LLC
Chambersburg PA
CBHW052022290426
44112CB00014B/2345